Supernova Advisor Teams

A PATHWAY TO EXCELLENCE

Curtis C. Brown, Jr.
Rob Knapp

WILEY

Published by John Wiley & Sons, Inc., Hoboken, New Jersey.

Published simultaneously in Canada.

For general information on our other products and services or for technical support, please contact our Customer Care Department within the United States at (800) 762–2974, outside the United States at (317) 572–3993, or fax (317) 572–4002.

Wiley publishes in a variety of print and electronic formats and by print-on-demand. Some material included with standard print versions of this book may not be included in e-books or in print-on-demand. If this book refers to media such as a CD or DVD that is not included in the version you purchased, you may download this material at http://booksupport.wiley .com. For more information about Wiley products, visit www.wiley.com.

Library of Congress Cataloging-in-Publication Data is Available:

ISBN 978-1-119-47745-7 (Hardcover)
ISBN 978-1-119-47792-1 (ePDF)
ISBN 978-1-119-47791-4 (ePub)

Cover Design: Wiley
Cover Image: © grindley78/iStockphoto

Printed in the United States of America

10 9 8 7 6 5 4 3 2 1

To my father, who spent 25 years in the US Army, two tours of duty in Vietnam, and who moved us from place to place and taught me perseverance and resilience. I remember a conversation later in life, when he said, "I'm sorry I wasn't able to do enough for you." I responded, "You gave me some important gifts that no one could ever take away, a sense of attitude, belief, and commitment." For all military veterans, I salute you!

To my mother, who was always there to provide encouragement when needed. You led one of my first teams, a group of cub scouts! I still remember the scout oath, which began with, "On my honor, I will do my best."

And to my wife and everyone who is battling cancer. Keep up the good fight and may God continue to bestow His blessing on all of you.

Curtis

To my daughter Courtney, who encouraged me to take the leap of faith and cross the invisible bridge 10 years ago and start Supernova Consulting group. She has acted as mentor, muse, and editor on much of my writing. To Greg Perry, who has been my editor for the last 10 years and tragically lost his life recently. If I was the brain of The Supernova Advisor, *he was the voice. His style, energy, writing skills, and constant encouragement will be missed. To Cindy Beuoy, who has constantly pushed our team at Supernova forward and held us accountable for our roles and responsibilities. Supernova would have been a fading star long ago without her support.*

Rob

Contents

Foreword

This book is about teams creating their "mojo" and becoming the best that they can be. The authors provide an easy road map or pathway for team success. If your team is challenged with performance or issues of dysfunction, this book has answers for you. Whether you are at the initial stages of forming your team, expanding your team, or looking to enhance the team's competencies, there is plenty to be gained by reading this book.

As we approach a new age of evolution in the financial services industry, old practice models are giving way to more dynamic and agile team-based models to enhance productivity and performance. Curtis Brown and Rob Knapp were always innovative and creative throughout their leadership careers at Merrill Lynch. I have known them personally for more than 30 years and have seen them evolve their thought leadership over the past three-and-a-half decades of industry experience. The age of the sole practice advisor is giving rise to advisor teams, which is a natural evolution for the industry.

The discussion of the Force Multiplier Effect provides thought leadership as to how a collaborative team model can amplify a team's capabilities. These strategies and tactics can ensure that teams can leverage strengths to counteract marketplace threats to their advisory business models.

Unlike many consultants, Brown's experience was shaped by training and skills developed managing and leading efforts for Merrill Lynch in Washington, DC; Michigan; New Jersey; California; and Florida and working in the C-suite for the chairman and president of Merrill Lynch. There we were reunited again while I was an executive vice president managing Global Systems and Operations for a firm that established its footprint in 58 countries. My own career spanned 40 years of private client experience as both a branch and complex manager as well as a regional director and later as an entrepreneur.

I gave Brown his first assignment as a resident vice president in Ann Arbor, Michigan. Our paths would cross many times throughout his illustrious career. Brown's leadership was recognized three times by senior management as one of the top executives in the firm and once as the number one executive as measured by six different strategic objectives. This was a feat that not many executives in the firm were able to accomplish. He views most of these accomplishments as attributable to forming and creating dynamic teams throughout his career. While on a special assignment working for the then chairman of Merrill Lynch, David Komansky, and then president, Herb Allison, Brown had the challenge of working with some of the brightest and most capable executives in the firm as well as being an interface with the company's board of directors.

Brown's view of advisory teams – from the small branch to large branches to regions and the executive suite – gives him the experience and insight to see issues from both an advisor and a leadership perspective.

Knapp also worked for me in the Midwest by managing many offices. He is a former managing director of Merrill Lynch and the architect of the Supernova model he developed with a team of financial advisors and leaders at Merrill Lynch. He is the author of *The Supernova Advisor,* which has received much critical acclaim in the industry and was the subject of a dissertation by graduate students at MIT and a case study by a Harvard University professor. Rob's passion for coaching talented individuals to reach exceptional levels of performance has solidified his reputation throughout the financial services sector as a visionary and creative leader. He created Supernova Consulting Group, LLC, with the purpose of improving the client experience worldwide. Rob's former managers are consistently recognized for their accomplishments in developing teams, serving clients, and generating revenue.

Brown and Knapp are "spot on" in their view that to embrace change one must first have the right attitude to step outside one's comfort zone. The authors characterize the industry challenges aptly: Price compression, changing regulatory environment, demanding clients, and technological disruption – all reasons for teams to "raise their game" in this hypercompetitive industry. They provide a steady flow of information, strategies, and tactics to help teams become more effective. At the end of each chapter the authors provide a call to action or team challenge to put thoughts and ideas into practical use.

The authors' use of real-world examples and experiences figure prominently as they tie in the practical application of team collaboration that a reader can understand. I particularly enjoyed the discussion around collaboration and how teams can obtain leverage by working together to accomplish an improved client experience. Brown and Knapp draw analogues outside the industry in their description of the precision of the Navy's flight demonstration team, Blue Angels, and a trauma surgery team.

Brown and Knapp offer up solutions to team dysfunction and identify the issues that impede team performance. If your team struggles with matters that impact performance, the authors present proven solutions to move your team forward.

Teams often struggle with leadership challenges; Brown and Knapp offer advice for improvement. Teams are like intrapreneurial businesses inside larger organizations, and the elements for building a practical business plan and strategy document are discussed in-depth. As demographic shifts occur in our industry, the authors make the case for adding diverse team members to avoid "groupthink" and take advantage of the opportunities associated with niche markets.

The authors devote an entire chapter to the manager/ leader. For managers responsible for coaching and developing teams, this book is a tremendous resource. The manager is responsible for creating the right environment for teams to thrive. The manager plays an integral role in helping teams leverage the capabilities of their firms. I suggest you give a copy of the book to your manager.

The overall message of the book is that teams can get better and become more effective, even in the face of so many challenges. Brown and Knapp have created a handbook on teaming that anyone contemplating forming a team or improving team performance should have in their repertoire of must-read books.

EDWARD L. GOLDBERG
Former EVP, Merrill Lynch
Managing Partner, Dix Hills, LLC

Preface

Rob Knapp's first book, *The Supernova Advisor*, provided great practical concepts for productivity improvement ideas for financial advisors. Most of those concepts revolve around advisor team improvement strategies. This book focuses specifically on team effectiveness strategies. It answers the question, "How do we continue to help teams be more effective?" Many of the concepts have materialized because of our firsthand experiences coaching and leading teams for more than 37 years at a major investment firm, entrepreneurial pursuits, and coaching financial advisors at many firms across the country.

We want to build on the training learned in *The Supernova Advisor* and help current advisor teams develop the strategies and tactics to become more efficient. When team members go through the program together, what emerges is a consensus view as to how a team can improve productivity and deliver its value proposition and improve the client experience.

Throughout this book we are sharing experiences gained by seeing teams both succeed and face many roadblocks during their journey to success, and productivity improvement as well as learning to deliver a client experience that went beyond a basic commodity experience. Our firsthand knowledge came from coaching several hundred teams over the past several decades, coupled with years of corporate experience being involved with teams being assembled without thought given to team alignment, business plans, or strategy. We experienced teams falling into dysfunctional traps without a framework or guidance to make midcourse corrections. This is a key focus of our consulting practice.

The motivation for the book came about after doing much research about teams and not finding a current book that addressed the issues that were more specific to financial advisor teams. However, many of the ideas and concepts discussed can go beyond organizational silos and provide relevance to other sales organizations.

We also discovered if we could get teams to capture the collective wisdom of their knowledge and experiences, they could improve their chances of success. The Wall Street culture, the one we grew up in, didn't foster collaboration and the Force Multiplier Effect described in Chapter 7, "Team Collaboration," to the best benefit of the team or the organizations that employed them. This isn't necessarily a knock on these organizations, however; the sole practice model was largely based on individual performance, not team performance, and, as such, you were rewarded accordingly. The former model didn't foster collaboration.

Chapter 15, "Wealth Management in the Digital Age," was a challenge to write due to the speed at which change and disruption is occurring in the financial services industry. Teams must consider that these changes are like a "sea of permanent white water" for those of you who have ever been rafting on the Colorado River and experienced the calm, the speed, and the turbulence associated with this type of adventure. Also, discussing diversity is a challenge given most people's proclivities to form teams with like-minded individuals without consideration given to exploring differences that might create improved performance.

Most of what was written comes from our collective experiences. However, there were numerous articles to be found online and many periodicals from well-known universities as well as many books that helped us frame the concepts. Some of the information simply came from discussions with financial advisors on teams over the years.

Teams are the principal building blocks of the strategy of successful organizations. The focus of your organization may be on service, quality, cost, value, speed, efficiency, performance, or any other similar goals, but teams remain the central methodology of most organizations in the private, nonprofit, and government sectors. While our focus is on financial advisor teams, there are many areas and discussion points that are applicable to teams outside the financial services industry.

The fact remains that when a team becomes more aligned, a commonality of direction emerges, and the individual energies harmonize. This way there is a shared vision as well as an understanding of how to complement each other's efforts. This is where the real leverage occurs.

Vertical teams and horizontal teams can transcend organizational silos and boundaries if properly focused and supported. Building collaborative teams can improve the client experience.

The financial services industry has become very challenging for a host of reasons. The role of the financial advisor has become increasingly more challenging because of several factors:

- Price and margin compression and an inability to raise prices require larger number of assets to increase productivity.
- The sole practitioner has limited scale to provide an elevated level of service and be knowledgeable or an expert on a range of strategies and products that clients need.
- Clients are demanding an above-average experience in a relationship that puts pressure on the sole practitioner advisor service models.
- The regulatory environment requires advisors to do a deeper dive in understanding client relationships as well as their goals and objectives.
- Digital advice channels that can scale in a price-competitive way have emerged.

In this new reality, advisors must build, lead, and manage their business through team dynamics. This goes beyond just an assembly of individuals thrown together because they like each other or have similar business strategies. More emphasis will need to be placed on creating the right team scenarios, coaching them, and providing the best opportunities for leverage and success. Supernova has decided to take team training and development to the next level by offering additional training for teams to improve productivity.

In 1965, Bruce Tuckman[1] identified five phases of team development as Storming, Forming, Norming, Performing, and Adjourning. Supernova focuses its training on team effectiveness strategies for advisors:

1. You must come to grips with your fears or inhibitors that hold you back. Write them down and then ask yourself, "What are the positive outcomes if I make the change?" Don't lead with the negative by asking, "What's the worst thing(s) that can happen to me?"
2. Remind yourself of your core values and dedication to helping others reach their dreams and goals. You must believe that when you wake up in the morning and look at yourself in the mirror, you are trying to do good for others.
3. It's okay to think about yourself and your family's quality of life. You can create balance for a win-win outcome.
4. Don't forget how far you've come. Recall those situations when you stepped out of your comfort zone and had positive outcomes. Take some solace that you have broken through barriers at other times during your life.
5. Don't go it alone. Get a coach, find mentors, and establish your personal advisory board. Sometimes a third party can help you through some of the challenges you might be facing. Seek feedback from people you can trust.

NOTE

1. Bruce Wayne Tuckman carried out research into the theory of group dynamics. In 1965, he published one of his theories called "Tuckman's stages of group development." In 1977, he added a fifth stage named Adjourning. According to the Tuckman theory of group development, there are four phases of group development: Forming, Storming, Norming, and Performing.

Acknowledgments

I have had the opportunity over three decades to work with a variety of professionals in both a corporate and nonprofit environment. Sometimes my role was leader and at times it was follower. People come into your life and provide inspiration. I choose to find the good in everyone. We are all the sum total of what we experience in life. I always tried to take a few golden nuggets from all those individuals I worked with over many years.

Finally, I want to acknowledge all the coaches who try to help individuals reach their true potential every day.

For those of you whom I have crossed paths with, I hope we touched each other in a special and positive way.

My mentors over the years are too numerous to mention. However, I would be remiss if I didn't name a few: David Komansky, former CEO of Merrill Lynch; Edward Goldberg, former EVP, Merrill Lynch; Jim Shoaf, former head of National Sales, Merrill Lynch; Ernie Moeglin, former district director, Merrill Lynch; Winthrop H. Smith, former EVP and head of Merrill Lynch International; Alan Sislen, Merrill Lynch; and Jim McCarthy and Andrew P. Edlemann, who gave me my first job at Merrill Lynch in San Francisco.

Some special thanks to Ed Goldberg for writing the Foreword. Thanks for being my friend.

Ronald Brown, PhD, gave me great insight to write a chapter about diversity and inclusion for teams.

Andre Campbell, MD, provided great content on shock trauma surgery teams.

Bruce Dillard, thanks for your service and guidance regarding the Navy's flight demonstration team.

Debra Frazier, thanks for sharing a valuable story.

Thanks to Cindy Beuoy at Supernova Consulting for your great ideas.

Also, thanks to Sydney LeBlanc for copyediting, catching my typos, and pushing me to completion of the manuscript.

Curtis

To all my coaches and leaders along the way, who have taught me the value of teamwork. To my tennis coaches, "Bud" Knapp (Dad), Jack Lynch, Phil Swanson, and Jim Leighton, who taught me the value of hard work, persistence, love of the game, patience, perseverance, and learning by coaching others.

To my naval flight instructors and commanding officers, who taught me the value of respecting all members of the flight crew, the value of all teammates' contributions, the importance of attention to detail, and the commitment to excellence at every level. That work, athletics, and the joy of learning and growing can go together to make you a better aviator. That you can learn as much from what not to do, as what to do.

To my mentors, leaders, bosses, and teammates at Merrill Lynch and Supernova, who taught me that with real focus and commitment you can achieve heights of success not even imagined. That nice guys can finish first and winning is a process that goes on forever. That commitment to excellence isn't just a slogan on a wall but a mantra to get up to every day. That if you instill the right values into your team, those values can live on after you in spite of difficult times and adversity.

Rob

Why Form a Team?

"By seizing the opportunities that disruption presents and leveraging hard times into greater success through outworking/outinnovating/outthinking and outworking everyone around you, this just might be the richest time of your life so far."

— Robin S. Sharma, Global Leadership Expert, Bestselling Author

In the financial services industry, the age of the sole practitioner advisor is a business model with many inherent challenges. The sole practitioner has been replaced by financial advisor teams that provide leverage to client relationships and can provide more than a commodity client experience. The key differentiating factor is for advisors to provide a service model that is unique and that focuses on the client first. Let's examine some of the trends and/or threats to the industry as well as an advisor's practice that fully support the rationale for creating effective teams.

Price Compression

So how did we get here? A little history is in order. In May 1975, brokerage industry commissions were deregulated. It brought new competitors into the market and basically broke up the monopoly on securities pricing. The downside to this free market pricing scenario is that the industry has not been able to raise prices since that time frame. Innovative firms adjusted by creating proprietary products that, for quite some time, eliminated any reason to raise prices. This was, in large part, because proprietary products had considerably higher fees or sales commissions associated with them. The industry was very innovative in generating new mutual funds, public partnerships, private placements, lending, and many hybrid products that helped to stem the tide of increasingly growing operating costs associated with running the business. Unfortunately, many products didn't live up to client expectations and there were inherent conflicts associated with this innovation.

With operating costs continuing to rise to the present day, financial advisor business models must evolve as well. Unlike many industries that pass on additional costs of doing business to the consumer, the financial services industry is challenged to use this strategy. Clients have the power to vote with their feet, walk away, and take their business to a host of competing organizations. Gone are the days where simple transactional business was a component of delivering an exceptional client experience. Price compression in the industry is one of the threats to doing business that requires financial advisors to transform their practices to deliver a value proposition based on advice and guidance.

The Dilemma I Faced

I (Curtis) recall as a branch manager taking on an assignment in the Northeast. The complex had four locations and approximately 50 financial advisors. On the surface, it was a very profitable complex. There were no teams in the office, and approximately 13 financial advisors controlled more than $13 billion in assets, a key driver of performance. Those advisors were all at least 55 years of age or older and potentially could face retirement in a few years. The potential loss of client relationships due to the retirement of these advisors and the lack of a quality service experience could also negatively impact branch office performance.

I fully expected I could lose substantial revenues in a two- to three-year time frame during my tenure due to turnovers, retirement, and other causes. Additionally, the return on assets was relatively low, at 0.04 percent. We had plenty of assets, but the client experience numbers were woefully low. I needed to find a solution to this dilemma!

We needed to help these advisors create the capacity for change as well as do a deeper dive with existing client relationships. Creating teams around these financial advisors to improve productivity as well as improve the client experience was important. Everyone could interview both internal and external advisor candidates. We established a simple profile by asking potential teams and team members who they would like to work with on a team, and then initiated and fostered interviews and meetings between individuals. In some cases, candidates who had great credentials, MBAs, former attorneys, business professionals, and certified public accountants (CPAs) were hired. When teams hire and/or onboard a new team member, they have a vested interest in the team member's success. Each team was required to develop a business plan and strategy document and receive ongoing coaching by a manager. The ongoing coaching was key to the success of teaming strategies. If bodies of people were just assembled together, the overall strategy would not have worked.

In discussions with teams it was understood that the firm was making an investment in their practice. It was explained that the person being hired would cost in compensation and benefits, close to $100,000. It became very clear, and the team understood the commitment that all parties would be making to ensure the success of the new team member (see Chapter 12, "Onboarding and Mentoring a New Team Member"). The team would make the final decision on hiring the new team member; it was never a forced relationship. There would be a two-year probationary period before the team member would achieve permanent status on the new team.

These new team members were also supported by going through a rigorous branch training program led by managers and experienced financial advisors. The overall impact was extremely positive, and it moved the office along in forming new team relationships.

The components of a team business plan and strategy document consisted of the following:

- Vision statement
- Mission statement
- SWOT analysis
- Goals
- Business forecast

The plans were comprehensive; however, these were the basic components. Meetings were scheduled with each team on a quarterly basis, and supplemental team-based training was instituted. We cannot underscore the importance of continued team-based training. There were times when team-based practice management sessions were scheduled. Successful teams from other branch offices were brought in to spend time coaching these teams. We would organize the office and run segmented training sessions based on an advisor's level of productivity and the developmental needs of each group. For teams at, or near, the $2 million in revenue level, we might have coaching sessions by either bringing in teams or visiting with teams at the $4 million or $7 million level. This was particularly helpful in enabling teams to modify behaviors and make productivity improvements. We wanted teams to believe they could accomplish stretch goals. Peer-to-peer meetings and training sessions fostered exponential learning, and the successful approaches reinforced positive team behaviors.

This, in turn, created an environment where the successful teams could mentor and share successful concepts with other financial advisor teams within the complex. "Success breeds success," as is commonly understood by many. Of course, creating a culture of teaming does take some work, as you will discover after you read more about team effectiveness strategies. The positive outcomes were that teams began collaborating with each other on specific client initiatives. If a team didn't have the expertise, they could collaborate with a team that was competent in a specific area, such as business financial services, pensions, or areas more specific to the ultra-high-net-worth clients. Decisions were made to take teaming to a new level by fostering collaboration and partnering within several business units and specialists. There were numerous specialists representing a considerable number of products and services. We made every effort to make them a part of the team in the office. They became collaborative team members supporting our client development and marketing efforts. These specialists were not made to feel like outsiders to what we were trying to accomplish. A discussion of this Force Multiplier Effect and collaborative business model occurs in a later chapter.

Sometimes it was necessary to intervene in conflict resolution or the restructuring of team agreements. And on rare occasions we were involved in team dissolutions. The complex grew to 135 financial advisors in three years. New hires were succeeding at a 90%-plus success rate. Turnover among financial advisors was almost nonexistent. Revenues and assets more than doubled within three years, with revenues approaching $100 million. While many of the quantitative results were significant, the impact to the culture and achievement of financial advisors was even more impactful.

If financial services firms want to have a positive impact on organic growth, team effectiveness strategies offer an excellent solution and approach. No one would ever consider forming a team and then walking away thinking that the work is done. When you have a group of talented individuals such as any professional sports team, the dynamic that separates the team is the leader/coach. Well-coached teams have greater chances to improve performance and succeed in a variety of environments.

Lessons Learned

What did we learn by creating an environment where more than 60% of the advisors were on a team? Merely putting people together as a cobbled-together solution will not work. Teams must have a unifying vision. There must be a team business plan with a delegation of duties and responsibilities for each team member. Teams must have working agendas as they approach each day. Communication strategies must be scheduled, and performance must be measured weekly. Teams must deal with common failure points. (Team dysfunctions are discussed later in Chapter 13, "Team Dysfunction: The Elephant in the Room.") Teams must achieve performance and leverage. One plus one must equal the equivalent of having three team members. There are a variety of team structures that can work. One size does not fit all. The potential benefits of improved productivity, improved client experience, and team satisfaction far outweigh the reasons not to form a team.

A research study on advisor teams conducted by the consulting firm of ClientWise and the investment management firm of Legg Mason (CWLM) in 2015 confirms this.[1] There were also many studies on teams during our careers at Merrill Lynch. The Merrill research pointed out the obvious: Teams are more productive than sole practitioners by huge margins. A few key points are worth noting in the CWLM study. The respondents came from wirehouses, hybrid registered investment advisors (RIAs), and RIAs.

- Forty-eight percent of teams had a written strategy plan.
- Fifty-nine percent had a written vision statement.
- Fifty-one percent had a statement of core values.
- Forty-eight percent indicated that having a written strategy plan was the most valuable tool for team success.
- Seventy-three percent had accountability for team goals.

It's clear that once teams can move past the forming, storming, and norming stages, they can then move toward performing and accountability for team-based goals. We must approach these statistics and evaluate teams on their capacity to increase or improve productivity. If you place two $500,000 producers together, you have a million-dollar team. The key is to leverage complementary strengths to achieve more significant revenues. Coaching must help determine a team's capacity to improve. It's more than just looking at the numbers and benchmarking a team's performance based on their length of service and/or peer comparisons.

NOTE

1. http://www.clientwise.com/blog/quantifying-the-value-of-successful-financial-advisory-teams.

CHAPTER 1

Stepping Outside of Your Comfort Zone

"In the end, we only regret the chances we didn't take, the relationships we were afraid to have, and the decisions we waited too long to make."

—Anonymous

As you embark on any change strategy from doing things the way you have always done them, you will need to start first with yourself and your attitude about change. This must happen before transformation can really take place. So let's spend some time discussing how to move forward before we move into some of the team strategies.

Let's face it, we all want to be comfortable in life. At times, factors such as managing change, reaching new levels of performance, and establishing stretch goals can be difficult, if not exhausting. After many years in this business, you want to feel you've arrived at a special place in life and can enjoy the fruits of your labor. Over time you fall into the comfort zone. Life can be repetitive and boring. You know what to expect at every turn. This leads to complacency, and for some of us it is easy to fall into a rut. You've heard the adage time and time again, "We are all creatures of habit." There's a lot of comfort in knowing your routines and what's around the corner. But sometimes these repetitive routines can be like boundaries that hold us back and keep us inwardly focused, thus keeping us from experiencing new things. When you have a set of predetermined activities and approaches that become second nature, you are then able to minimize stress and risk. The comfort zone is a state of mental security that provides regular happiness and low anxiety. The problem is that this state—if prolonged—will keep you from feeling challenged and experiencing new things.

I (Curtis) recall growing up as a "military brat" and moving eight times. It seemed as soon as I was getting comfortable with my environment, the school, friends, surroundings, and so on, it was time to move again. This carried into my adult life with an additional seven corporate moves. I'm not knocking a stable environment and those who have lifelong childhood friends and know the neighborhood grocer. But each time I moved I had to adjust to a different environment, a new culture, and establish new relationships. This was to be my foundation of dealing with change, taking new risks, and understanding fundamentally that change won't kill you – it might even be good for you. I try to treat each move as a new adventure and as an opportunity to meet new people and explore an unfamiliar environment.

One fundamental fact about venturing into the unknown and trying new things as a financial advisor (FA) is the fear associated with reaching new heights of performance. You've been successful, a great family provider, you serve on a couple of non-profit boards, and maybe coach your kid's sports team in your spare time. In the winter you go skiing, and during the summer you visit the lake or the beach. You've grown accustomed to this life and the pattern, and on the surface, it feels pretty good. However, something is missing. You know what it is: You could be doing more or doing better. But stepping outside your comfort zone seems risky, scary, and downright uncomfortable. Ask yourself this fundamental question and be honest: "What's the one or two biggest impediments to breaking out of your comfort zone?" If you answered me, me, and me, well then, you are well on your way to breaking out of your comfort zone. It's not your boss, your firm, family, or resources that are holding you back!

Stretching Beyond Your Comfort Zone

Our obsession with comfort can haunt us and keep us from realizing our full potential, not to mention some new and exciting adventures we might miss out on. Be careful of tried-and-true benchmarks or comparisons. Expressions like, "I'm outperforming everyone in my office"; "I'm number one in my district"; "I'm highly ranked in my class"; and "I'm making more than I ever have before." Sure, be proud of your accomplishments and achievements; however, set benchmarks that stretch you beyond your comfort zone.

When we get comfortable in the "zone," it is like a gravitational pull that moves us toward what is fun and easy, rather than toward what is difficult, challenging, and goal achieving. Remember the teacher, the coach, your parent, or maybe that drill instructor who pushed you beyond your boundaries and so-called limitations? It wasn't easy going through it; however, you succeeded and went on to higher levels of performance. You had to first let go of the chains that bound you. For the most part, these chains were mental. Once you break through, you feel elation and accomplishment. That's a feeling that you must play back in your mind from time to time. It gives us strength.

It's not all about success; it's about the journey, and sometimes there are setbacks along the way. There are no guarantees, and sometimes we get derailed. The thrill comes when we get back up and try again and, later, overcome the obstacles that hinder our success.

Let's recall Bethany Hamilton, a surfer at 13, who lost her arm and nearly lost her life in a vicious shark attack in 2003 in Kauai. One month later she was back on her surfboard with a determined spirit and positive attitude. Two years later she won first place in the Explorer Women's Division of the NSSA National Championships.

How about another familiar name, Dr. Seuss, who wrote 46 books that sold more than 200 million copies. His first book (*And to Think That I Saw It on Mulberry Street*) was reportedly rejected by 28 publishers before being published. His persistence in the face of rejection paid off. Big time.

One of my favorite stories is about a person who literally ran out of his comfort zone – athlete, physician, and academic, Roger Bannister. People had been trying to break the four-minute mile since the time of ancient Greece. Everyone believed that it was physiologically impossible for a human to run a mile in four minutes. Experts said the bone structure was inadequate and that lung capacity wouldn't allow it. Soon after Bannister broke the four-minute mile in 1954, 37 other runners broke the four-minute barrier. The following year, 300 runners broke the four-minute mile barrier.

The themes in the previous examples reveal true human breakthroughs in attitude. There are many examples of people doing extraordinary things to overcome adversity and step outside their comfort zones. You can get a little inspiration by reading stories about human potential to break through life's challenges from time to time.

It takes tenacity and courage to embark on a personal change strategy or reinvention, as some say. The first has to do with *attitude.* A positive attitude will allow you to face the challenges of everyday life. It's your state of mind and your outlook and view on things. The second component to your change strategy is your *belief* in yourself and what you're doing. It's not arrogance, it's confidence. The third component is *commitment.* When you are committed to something, you make no excuses, the debate is over, and there is no more lengthy analysis, just action.

Today, change the words from "I'm not comfortable doing that" to "My life experiences have prepared me to accept new and exciting challenges."

Characteristics of Successful Teams

What are the characteristics of successful teams? According to *The Wisdom of Teams* by Jon R. Kazenbach and Douglas K. Smith,[1] and *The Human Side of Enterprise* by Douglas MacGregor,[2] there are 11 characteristics of effective teams:

1. **There is a clear unity of purpose.** There is free discussion of the objectives until members could commit themselves to them; the objectives are meaningful to each group member.
2. **The group is self-conscious about its own operations.** The group has taken time to explicitly discuss group

process – how the group will function to achieve its objectives. The group has a clear, explicit, and mutually agreed-upon approach: Mechanics, norms, expectations, rules, and so on. Frequently, it will stop to examine how well it is doing or what may be interfering with its operation. Whatever the problem may be, it gets open discussion and a solution found.

3. **The group has set clear and demanding performance goals.** The team has performance goals that translate into well-defined concrete milestones against which it measures itself. The team defines and achieves a continuous series of "small wins" along the way to larger goals.

4. **The atmosphere tends to be informal, comfortable, relaxed.** There are no obvious tensions; a working atmosphere is created in which team members are involved and interested.

5. **There is a lot of discussion in which virtually everyone participates.** But it remains pertinent to the purpose of the group. If discussion gets off track, someone will bring it back in short order. The members listen to each other. Every idea is given a hearing. People are not afraid of appearing foolish by putting forth a creative thought, even if it seems extreme.

6. **People are free in expressing their feelings as well as their ideas.** If individual team members fear retribution, unwarranted criticism, or being cast in a negative light, or adverse impact to their compensation, they will not speak up. Leadership must determine if it's going to be a culture where everyone goes along or if there is an opportunity for healthy contentious discussion.

7. **There is disagreement, and this is viewed as good.** Disagreements are not suppressed or overridden by premature group action. The reasons are carefully examined, and the team seeks to resolve them rather than dominate the dissenter. Dissenters are not trying to dominate the group; they have a genuine difference

of opinion. If there are basic disagreements that cannot be resolved, the team figures out a way to live with them without letting them block its efforts.

8. **Most decisions are made at a point where there is general agreement.** However, those who disagree with the general agreement of the team do not keep their opposition private and let an apparent consensus mask their disagreement. The group does not accept a simple majority as a proper basis for action.

9. **Everyone carries his or her own weight.** Each team member meets or exceeds the expectations of other team members. Everyone is respectful of the mechanics of the team: Arriving on time, coming to meetings prepared, completing agreed-on tasks on time, and so on. When action is taken, clear assignments are made (who-what-when) and willingly accepted and completed by each team member.

10. **Criticism is frequent, frank, and relatively comfortable.** The criticism has a constructive flavor oriented toward removing an obstacle that faces the team.

11. **The leadership of the group shifts from time to time.** The issue is not who controls but how to get the job done.

If you are looking to build a talented team, one doesn't have to look very far. I'm reminded of the great John Wooden, basketball coach at UCLA. He set the standard for great coaches and leadership. He coached his teams to 10 NCAA national basketball championships in a 12-year period – seven in a row! In the corporate world, Jack Welch, the chairman and CEO of General Electric between 1981 and 2001, propelled the company's value, and GE stocks went up 4,000%, making it the most valuable corporation in the world at the time during his tenure. These leaders built long-lasting sustainable teams. There was a great interest and a passion for people development.

> ## Team Challenge
>
> Have each team member score the team on the 11 characteristics previously discussed on a scale of 1 (lowest) to 5 (highest). Then bring the team together and discuss the scores and areas for team improvement.

NOTES

1. Jon R. Kazenbach and Douglas K. Smith, *The Wisdom of the Teams* (Boston, MA: Harvard Business Review Press, 1992).
2. Douglas MacGregor, *The Human Side of Enterprise* (New York: McGraw-Hill, 2005).

2

Distinct Types of Teams

"Individual commitment to a group effort – that is what makes a team work, a company work, a society work, a civilization work."

—Vince Lombardi

T here are several types of advisor teams:

- Vertical team
- Horizontal team
- Specialty team
- Virtual team
- Multicultural and diverse teams

But teams fall into two basic types: Vertically integrated teams and horizontal teams. The basic definitions follow.

A **vertical team** might have a senior producer/partner, a junior producer, and a client associate/administrative assistant. A **horizontal team** may consist of three financial advisors. They may be somewhat equal in productivity, and then they have one or two client associates or administrative assistants working with them. Let's discuss them in more detail now:

- **Vertical team:** The vertical team has a key person who is operating under one production member who is fully in charge, in addition to a junior financial advisor or partner working on the team, and one client associate.
- **Horizontal team:** In the horizontal team, the members delegate duties and responsibilities and each of the three or more people on the team share power to a certain extent – specifically, decision making that takes place is made by three people, making it a "flatter" organizational

team. They make decisions on strategy and on the technical products and services they are utilizing. They pool their resources, both from an asset management standpoint and from a production standpoint, and then they may equally share in payouts. It can differ by percentages. For example, one team member might be at 40% of total team production, and another team member might be equal at 40%, but the third team member might have a 20% share. There could also be various permutations like a third, a third, a third in terms of the revenue-sharing arrangement.

How do those two teams differ? Primarily, in the decision-making process. The senior producer on the vertical team is making most of the decisions for that team. He or she is setting forth all the strategy and tactical plans, and the other team members follow the lead of the senior advisor. This doesn't always happen, however; in most cases, the senior advisor on the team makes the final decisions. In smaller vertical teams, the delegation of duties and responsibilities is limited. Team members may have a variety of functional responsibilities as well as expertise. In horizontal teams, each team member may be involved in decision making. Horizontal teams tend to take more of a consensus view as to decision making and the overall direction of the team. Since there tends to be three or more advisors on a horizontal team, power, authority, and decisions are shared by each of the team members. A horizontal team is usually formed when one team member decides to bring people onto the team that have a variety of functional capabilities. One team member might focus on lending and liability management solutions for clients. Another team member might focus on investment solutions for clients. The third team member might focus on financial, estate planning, and insurance solutions. It's when teams leverage their functional expertise that they provide clients a better experience.

The Client Experience: More About Your Team Differentiation

An important key to market differentiation is providing value-added capabilities that improve the client experience. Let's address 10 things that will differentiate your team:

1. **Clients want more than a commodity experience.** Clients want an experience that keeps them coming back. There are many places we all come back to visit even if there is a better-priced alternative. None of us want to pay for an unpleasant experience. Show (don't tell) them your team's value by practicing it consistently.

2. **Clients want to know they can trust you.** Clients want to be able to trust and rely on you. Solving their problems within 24 hours should be your mantra. If you do what you say you'll do, then your clients will come to trust you. Trust is a primary ingredient for the sustainability of your team and your practice.

3. **The client experience must be consistent.** Amazon, Ritz Carlton, American Express, Disney, and Coke all create a standard of repeat business and long-term relationships. Think about it—revenues are enhanced when clients return and take advantage of your other services! Your team members should embrace this concept.

4. **You must offer an elevated level of client engagement.** An elevated level of engagement means that you are responsive to clients and take time to understand what they want; confirm that they are on track; and communicate promptly when things don't go as planned. This is an emotional attachment that takes place over time; it can't be rushed, and it is worth all the time in the world to engage your clients properly.

5. **Clients are people with real emotions; therefore, the experience must be on an emotional level.** "Behavioral psychologists have long argued that only 30 percent of human decisions and behaviors are actually driven by rational considerations. This means that more than 70 percent of consumer loyalty and spending decisions are based on emotional factors."[1] We believe that business is first a meeting of the hearts and then it becomes a meeting of the minds.

6. **A positive client experience must be deliberate and cannot happen by accident.** Creating a positive client experience must be part of your overall strategy for your business. You can plan for increasing assets and revenue per relationship, and define the most appropriate product or service, but you must incorporate a plan for an overall positive client experience. This cannot happen by accident. Your clients will comprehend and appreciate the effort you put into creating a positive experience for them.

7. **The customer experience must deliver value and be easy, noncomplicated, and enjoyable.** Deliver value, make it easy to do business with you, and make it an enjoyable experience – three simple, yet crucial, ingredients for the most positive client experience.

8. **Meet, set, and define client expectations to create a positive interactive experience. A positive experience = loyalty.** Financial advisors must take a leadership role and walk the client through a discovery process and set and define expectations. This experience creates loyalty and contributes to the sustainability of your practice as well as to the overall value of your team.

9. **Improve the client experience as a competitive differentiator.** There are two areas of financial services that are a commodity (meaning you can get it anywhere). One is products or services, and the other is information. Your value is positively impacted by understanding how the information impacts the client positively or negatively. If you improve the client

experience, you can distance yourself from other competitors. Make sure that your clients understand that your team delivers a comprehensive client experience. This includes multigenerational planning and full implementation of the plan through 12-4-2 service (meaning interacting with the clients a minimum of once a month, with four of those contacts being reviews and two of those reviews being in-person meetings) and rapid response to the client's concerns (one-hour response, 24-hour resolution). This is the Supernova service model.

10. **Listen to your clients and their needs.** A disgruntled consumer will tell anywhere from 9 to 15 people about their unpleasant experience. About 13% of disgruntled customers tell more than 20 people.[2] It takes 12 positive service experiences to make up for one negative experience.[3] When meeting with clients, let them talk, and show your concern and appreciation by really listening to them and reacting when appropriate.

Who Does What?

One team member may have delegated duties and responsibilities for which he or she is accountable. All team members should participate in putting forth the strategies for the team and client acquisition in terms of measurement. Teams can define roles and responsibilities and accountabilities around specific strategies such as client acquisition, annuitized or fee-based income, portfolio management, estate planning, and financial plan implementation. A host of both strategic and tactical activities can be delegated to each team member.

The client associates or administrative assistants, on the other hand, have delegated responsibilities. They may be responsible for some client interface activities and problem resolution on the team from an administrative point of view. But they would also be responsible for scheduling of all prospect appointments, client appointments, client reviews, and more. The client associate becomes the face of the team and is the director of the team's operations and brand. A clear example of this is when you walk into a doctor's office. You are intercepted by a receptionist or administrative assistant who pulls your file before you see the doctor. This person schedules all appointments and manages all follow-up meetings and appointments, not the doctor.

Other Types of Teams

In addition to the vertical and the horizontal teams, there are several other types, for example, the specialty team, virtual team, and multicultural and diverse teams. The specialty team is either vertically integrated or it is a horizontal team that chooses to be very specific in what they specialize in as well as what they offer to a niche market. This may be a team that strictly focuses on nonprofit clients and nonprofit institutions and endowments. It's a specialized niche within their operating environments. They are creating specialized niche markets.

A virtual team might be a vertical or a horizontal team that pulls in a skilled advisor who is not an official member of the team that might be an expert in the retirement plans area, for example. When the team is working with either the pension or retirement plan and does not have the expertise, they may reach outside the team for specialized expertise. Let's say that an advisor has specialized institutional money management expertise and another team has an institutional relationship they're not familiar with; they may call in the specialist person to participate in a meeting on the topic with a prospect. It brings that expertise to bear on that prospective client relationship. Often, advisors or teams will come across opportunities they are not familiar with, and collaborating or working with a virtual team member may make perfect sense.

In many markets, multicultural/diverse teams can have various cultural dynamics, perhaps with Hispanics, African Americans, South Asian Indians, and other ethnicities. For example, in San Francisco 112 different languages are spoken. If you're interested in pursuing those markets, it would be helpful to have an advisor on the team who has that dimension to help cultivate business and relationships in those communities. It could be someone who is a part of that culture or perhaps has a language proficiency in working with that culture. The day where everybody on a team looks the same and thinks the same is evolving, and it may not maximize the effectiveness in terms of cultivating the emergence of a potential revenue stream that might exist within these other cultural environments. Also, another benefit is that many small businesses and institutions want to work with diverse teams.

Another thought is that, as a diverse team, you will have assembled people who look at a problem just a little bit differently, see an opportunity a little bit differently, and are diverse in ideas and thought. We discuss this in more detail in Chapter 16, "Diverse Teams and Niche Markets".

Figure 2.1 is a vertical collaborative team, and the advisor is the centerpiece of this collaboration. But this individual might collaborate with his marketing group. He may collaborate with his branch manager or with an advisor that brings a certain niche expertise outside of the competency of that team. Collaboration is leverage. For example, some firms have a private wealth group, and the advisor has the relationship with the CEO. The private wealth collaboration might bring retention and some specialized institutional capabilities that haven't been brought to that CEO and his company. And that's where collaboration gives this team what I call the "Force Multiplier," which we will discuss in detail later in Chapter 7, "Team Collaboration."

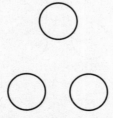

Figure 2.1   A vertical team with a senior advisor, junior advisor, and client associate.

Which Team Structure Do You Need? A, B, C, D, or E?

You don't just suddenly decide on a structure. We believe the team formation is all part of an evolution. Part of the dynamic of a team formation is to find people that you feel comfortable or compatible working with, that bring disparate viewpoints and skill sets that may need to evolve as well. You also need to decide on your team agreement and the niche markets you're going to prospect for client acquisition. Oftentimes, team formation begins with a senior producer establishing a relationship with a junior advisor who might eventually become an equity partner on the team.

As the team's production and revenue stream improve and new markets are contemplated, then the expansion of the team might go from Figure 2.1 to Figure 2.2. And then, once the

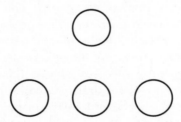

Figure 2.2   A vertical team, with two junior advisors and one client associate.

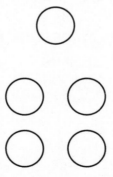

Figure 2.3   A vertical team, with two junior advisors and two client associates.

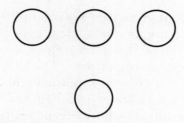

Figure 2.4 A horizontal team with three advisors and one client associate.

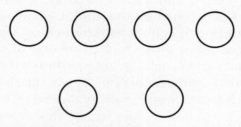

Figure 2.5 A horizontal team with four advisors and two client associates.

level of revenue and capacity starts to change, you're expanding the business and you might go to Figure 2.3 or something even more elaborate such as illustrated in Figures 2.4 and 2.5. Of course, there can be many permutations of advisor teams as well as permutations of responsibilities and titles that coincide with those accountabilities as well.

The Evolution of Team Business Models

Teams have a way of evolving based on market approaches, revenue growth and, of course, the increasing demands and acquisition of clients. And part of the evolution is based on how much a sole practitioner can handle in terms of workload. You see, a sole practitioner must have client-facing time and time for administration, researching ideas, implementing client strategies, client reviews, and more. When you start putting together all the things that need to be done and how much time is left for prospecting and generating new business, you will need a partner. If you want to take a holistic approach with clients and provide the level of a client experience that's more than a commodity experience, then there are more reasons to take on a team member or partner.

Team models can grow in sophistication and can become quite elaborate. We have come across 10- and 30-person teams. These teams have more elaborate budgets, marketing strategies, compensation systems, and specialties. For all intents and purposes, they are intrapreneurial groups within larger firms or entrepreneurial groups in an independent business model. The larger the team, the more sophisticated management and leadership strategies that must be instituted.

While these teams grow in structure and business performance, they have their challenges as well: Personnel challenges, making sure that team members are cast in the right roles, performance measurement, and strategic alignment, to name a few. In the independent business model, the challenges are managing sales and marketing efforts, managing the cash flow of the business, compliance posture, the strategic deployment of technology, and human resources management.

Team Challenge

Analyze your team's current business structure. Is it optimized for high performance? If you are thinking about establishing a team, begin to set a plan in place.

NOTES

1. http://www.circles.com/docs/CE%20Whitepaper_Engagement _071410.pdf.
2. White House Office of Consumer Affairs, Washington, DC.
3. Ruby Newell-Legner, "Understanding Customers." http:// ww2.glance.net/wp-content/uploads/2015/07/Counting-the -customer_-Glance_eBook-4.pdf.

3

Team Effectiveness

"Teamwork is the ability to work together toward a common vision. The ability to direct individual accomplishments toward organizational objectives. It is the fuel that allows common people to attain uncommon results."

—Andrew Carnegie

Effective teams operate like a business and incorporate small business owner–like processes.

Some teams may manage up to $500 million or more in assets, and some teams we've worked with have had several billion dollars in assets under management and generated millions of dollars in revenues. For all intents and purposes, they can be characterized as small businesses. If you were running a small business and you wanted to take it to another level, then doing a **SWOT analysis** (detailed in the SWOT Analysis section; in Figure 3.1 we provide a template for this purpose) makes a lot of sense. It's all a part of creating your team-based business plan. Sometimes a team comes together with assemblies of people, meaning they come together to form a team, but they still operate independently as individual advisors and they don't get the maximum leverage that we talked about in Chapter 2, "Distinct Types of Teams." They are moving in many different directions without alignment and a cohesive strategy. These teams seem to struggle with growth initiatives, client acquisition, their service models, and taking a holistic view of a client's needs. The client experience becomes just a commodity experience, and the team doesn't differentiate itself from other advisors.

The team's leader or business coach then needs to take the team's energy and organize it, package it, so that all members are like-minded and focused on strategies to be most effective. When we say like-minded, that isn't to say that differences of opinion and thought aren't appreciated as vital characteristics

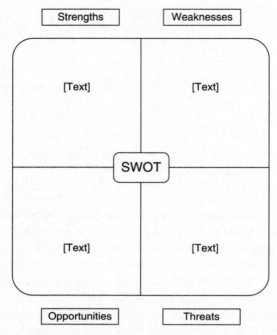

Figure 3.1 SWOT template.

that enable teams to succeed. With the SWOT analysis, it's important to do an assessment of your team's strengths. Once you understand the capabilities of each of the team members, you can then determine what differentiates your team from others and delivers the exceptional client experience that we have previously discussed.

Financial advisors need to understand what will stand in the way of their team's being highly successful. What keeps the team from accomplishing their mission? Have you made certain that the members have specific areas of expertise and capabilities that are collectively or holistically understood to really allow the team to move forward?

We recommend that the team complete an assessment to better understand their weaknesses and then decide how to respond to any developmental needs or challenges. Do you want to recruit another team member? Do you send a team member to a specialized training program to acquire much-needed skills? Do you want to create a partner relationship with another advisor team member to shore up those weaknesses? You're going to analyze revenue reports or other types of business reports and any performance data on the team and the team members – and that will allow you to really understand what gaps exist that need to be remedied. What are the barriers that stand in the way of the team's being successful? Who is willing to enthusiastically endorse you to be introduced to a prospective client, which will contribute to your client acquisition initiative? We believe that obtaining personal introductions leads to acquiring more clients.

That's the overall purpose of conducting the SWOT analysis. If this is just an exercise in futility and the team does not apply action items or initiatives for improvement, then the exercise becomes a team failure point. You must take the exercise (i.e., SWOT) and transform the team's analysis into actions and initiatives. Teams can talk about what they need to do in perpetuity, but if they don't translate this into action and determine who's going to be accountable and responsible, the team may fail. The lead person or team leader is leading the charge and monitoring the progress, and they are responsible for holding the team accountable for results. The team also needs a concise business plan document for review, alignment, and monitoring of progress toward goals.

Sometimes, team members are moving in so many different directions that it creates dysfunction, and that is why teams really need to take a half day, go through the process, and ultimately decide, "Hey, what do we stand for? What's our process? What are our strengths, weaknesses, and opportunities? What are our goals? Are we monitoring our progress with the goals that we set out to do?" Otherwise, teams can become stagnant and fall prey to complacency. There are plenty of examples of complacency in the business world. The "street," so to speak, is littered with companies that have failed to evolve or change their approaches or business models. Blockbuster Video and others failed due to disintermediation by online streaming by the likes of Netflix and video on demand offered by cable companies. Then there is the example of Eastman Kodak, which lost ground to digital cameras and smartphones with camera and video capabilities. Then, of course, there's Sears, which lost ground to Kmart, Walmart, and the online shift in consumer behavior.

The threats of price compression, changes in the regulatory environment, strong and/or flat markets, markets that are very volatile, and technological advances can all disrupt ways of doing business. In the face of these market threats, teams must challenge themselves in terms of retaining client relationships. The team environment coupled with technology can be a potent force multiplier.

Bringing Your Team Closer Together

When your team members have discussions about these challenges or other tasks they are dealing with at the time, it always helps to bring them closer together. If they're solving some of these problems together, then each member will bring something to the table for the benefit of the team. The key is to schedule time for team huddles, team meetings, and team evaluations of their performance. Teams should take a time-out to step back for a moment and assess their progress, internal relationships with one another, and the external relationships with their clients.

Ask these questions:

- How are we doing as a team?
- Looking at this road map that we put together – our business plan – are we paying attention to it?
- Are we making progress?
- Are there some shortcomings?
- Do we need to change course in any of the team strategies?
- Do we need to update our plan?

Think about it. These are some of the questions you are using in your discussions with your clients! We are suggesting you do the same things with your team members. Ask questions of your team: "Are we on target? Have we had setbacks? Do we need to make revisions? How has your life changed since the last time we talked or visited? Have you had events like a birth or a death, a divorce, eldercare for parents? Do we need to make some adjustments?"

There are opportunities for the team to do exceedingly well, and these solutions all become part of an action plan. It becomes part of the overall strategy of the team to decide the impact that they want to have on their business and to whom they will be delegating responsibilities. Who is the team going to hold accountable to make sure that action items are accomplished for execution? That is all part of a business plan or action plan. Some advisors don't believe they need one or don't know how to develop one. Teams don't understand how important it is, or they are overwhelmed with their day-to-day activities of assisting and helping clients. Teams that we coach often feel, at times, as though they are "drinking water from the fire hose."

A team needs help with streamlining and improving its business so members are better organized. This is where a planning template can help. It's no longer just about putting together two or three bodies and calling yourself a team. It's about taking the team to an additional level of effectiveness and performance.

We work with many teams that struggle with organization. Disorganization is what we call the steady creep of distractions and the lack of processes that begin to undermine team effectiveness. Issues of too many clients, lack of team structure, and administrative overload take a toll on their business.

When we cover the chapter outlining the five dysfunctions of a team, a lot can be learned. (See Chapter 13: "Team Dysfunction: The Elephant in the Room.") For example, members' reluctance to be vulnerable to one another or a peer conflict lead to suboptimal decision making. Perhaps a team member tries to make the required changes that are necessary for team success, but the team doesn't bring it up because they don't want the conflict. Now, let's look at the SWOT analysis by way of review.

SWOT Analysis

Let's review the process called a SWOT analysis of your team. **SWOT is an acronym for strengths, weaknesses, opportunities, and threats.** Strengths (S) and weaknesses (W) are internal factors over which you have some measure of control. Also, opportunities (O) and threats (T) are external factors over which you have essentially no control.[1]

Strengths are the capabilities of each of your team members. It's the capacity that differentiates your team from others that gives you special advantages in delivering an exceptional client experience. For some teams, it's their holistic approach to planning and/or product knowledge. It could be an ability to deliver comprehensive strategies for clients. It may be specialized capabilities in dealing with niche markets. What are the key strengths of your team and how do they positively impact team performance? What have your clients told you that you are especially good at?

Weaknesses are the characteristics that stand in the team's way or inhibit the team from accomplishing its mission. Perhaps asset growth and productivity has slowed. There may be issues regarding organization, specialized capabilities, not raising asset thresholds, or communication among team members. What are the weaknesses that impact your team, and what are you doing to address them?

Opportunities may exist for the team to gather more affluent clients and to improve the service capabilities of existing clients. Perhaps clients are unaware of your additional product offerings and the team needs to manage client contact and agendas more efficiently. What would it mean for the team if it could capitalize on the opportunities that exist for the team now?

Threats arise externally and can impact team performance. They are also beyond the team's control. These may be changes in the regulatory environment or competitive price compression on products and services. The economic environment can impact investments and investment strategies. Technology can disrupt previous ways of doing business. What is your team doing to combat some of these threats that exist today?

Rationale

This process will help teams identify their core competencies and build on their strengths while reversing weaknesses. It will help teams capitalize on opportunities and develop responses to threats to their team's business and productivity. This team discussion will help bring teams closer together to solve important problems or challenges facing the team. See the SWOT template in Figure 3.1.

Team Challenge

Have a team meeting and do a SWOT analysis and answer some of the questions identified earlier. Feel free to use the template. This will be added to your team's playbook or business plan. Does your team have a working business plan document? Once developed, the team will review their playbook monthly and determine if it is on track with the team's strategic and tactical plans. Appoint a scribe and take notes on an easel pad. Debate each quadrant and work toward a consensus view.

NOTE

1. http://managementstudyguide.com/swot-analysis.htm.

CHAPTER 4

Leadership Styles/Leading the Team

"The way a team plays as a whole determines its success. You may have the greatest bunch of individual stars in the world, but if they don't play together, the club won't be worth a dime."

—Babe Ruth

I n this chapter, we cover leadership styles. In the sole practitioner model (no team, advisor acting alone), you only needed to be concerned about yourself and your clients. Team leadership, however, requires so much more effort to leverage success; it shouldn't be overwhelming if done right because the benefits and rewards are substantial.

Rationale

You need to understand how these styles can positively or negatively impact your team performance and success.

There is a fundamental difference between leadership and management, based on writings by management consultant and author Peter Drucker.

According to Drucker:

> Manager and leader are two completely distinct roles, although we often use the terms interchangeably. Managers are facilitators of their team members' success. They ensure that their people have everything they need to be productive and successful; that they're well-trained, happy and have minimal roadblocks in their path; that they're

being groomed for the next level; that they are recognized for impressive performance and coached through their challenges.[1]

Team leaders are de facto managers of significant practices in most cases. Drucker continues:

> Conversely, a leader can be anyone on the team who has a talent, who is creatively thinking out of the box and has a great idea, who has experience in a certain aspect of the business or project that can prove useful to the manager and the team. A leader leads based on strengths, not titles."[2]

Psychologist and best-selling author Daniel Goleman's "Leadership That Gets Results," a landmark 2000 *Harvard Business Review* study, did research on more than 3,000 managers and defined six leadership styles. He further indicated that a manager's leadership style was responsible for **30%** of the organization's bottom line results.[3] We believe leadership on teams can have comparable results.

Drucker identified the emergence of the "knowledge worker" and the profound differences that would impact the way business was organized. With the rise of the knowledge worker, "One does not 'manage' people," Drucker wrote. "The task is to lead people. And the goal is to make productive the specific strengths and knowledge of every individual."[4]

We see managers assigning tasks, delegating duties and responsibilities, organizing, planning, and controlling. The leaders of teams provide inspiration and motivation, and rally team members around a common purpose. The leader helps to bring out the best in people. We see teams break down when there is no clearly defined leadership. We see an assembly of people very busy moving in many different directions with a lack of focus. The successful teams we see are driven toward a common purpose, with the team leader providing encouragement and inspiring confidence.

Successful and effective leaders and managers must do the same things. They need to set direction for followers and the organization, motivate, develop good working relationships with followers, be positive role models, and focus on goals.[5] In this book, let's change the term from *followers* to *team members,* which describes the vision of a cohesive group of people bound by a common purpose, values, and mission. The leader inspires his fellow members toward team effectiveness and successful mission accomplishment. If left to their own devices, people will set out in different directions to accomplish what they think is best for them and not necessarily what might be best for the team.

But in the new economy, where value comes increasingly from the knowledge of people, and where workers are no longer undifferentiated cogs in an industrial machine, management and leadership are not easily separated. People look to their managers, not just to assign them a task but to define for them a purpose. And managers must organize workers, not just to maximize efficiency but to nurture skills, develop talent, and inspire results.[6] We believe this holds true for teams as well, and therefore the term *manager* can be replaced with the term *team leader.*

The Leaderless Team

We often experience what can be defined as leaderless teams. No team member is taking responsibility, held accountable, or establishing the agenda for the team. On the surface, team members are so busy doing the work that is necessary to serve clients and earn a living that many elements that can truly make the team a great team go unchecked. Someone must clarify the team's purpose, organize the team around activities that get results, and help define the team's goals and agendas. The leader of the team must be able to share power, delegate duties and responsibilities, and help the team organize its work around a defined business plan. The team leader must challenge the team to meet performance goals and deadlines.

Most advisors do not come into the business with backgrounds in managing and leading "knowledge workers." This is not a reflection on their abilities; it's an activity that advisors were not either hired or trained to do. However, they just need to learn the behaviors necessary to be effective team leaders and team members.

Effective teams value the opinions of each team member, welcome input and innovative ideas, and value contentious discussion, as long as respect for the individual is maintained.

Let's examine six leadership styles and how they impact team performance.

1. **The pacesetting leader** needs a quick turnaround. If there is a crisis to deal with, this leader wants things done in a specific and urgent way. The team may be mobilizing for a very significant presentation with meaningful revenue and assets at stake. This style cannot work in a prolonged way because every project can't be a crisis. People on teams will burn out quickly under the pressure. This style can negatively impact creativity and innovation.

2. **The authoritative leader** can rally people around a common vision, mission, and goals. This leader can be inspirational; however, this style can begin to wane if the team has several experts that are just as smart as the team leader. Differences of opinion may cause conflict. It's important to respect differences and allow a consensus view to determine the outcome of a problem or solution. This leader must remind people at the end of the day that a decision must be made. Tension can occur when this leader adopts a "my way or the highway" type of demeanor. This leader takes the position that all the strategies and promising ideas reside in his/her domain.

3. **The affiliative leader** is an emotional leader who creates bonds with the members of the team. If the team has been through a cycle of stress or trauma, this leader can provide a healing nature. This is not a style that is used

for prolonged periods of time. It may cause the team to lose focus and direction or mission clarity. The loss of a major client, product failure, or a team member, for example, can create stress among team members. Team members must heal their wounds and move on. This leader recognizes the emotional state of the team and can help move the team forward. We are all reminded that setbacks do occur and as quickly as we can heal and move forward, better times will be forthcoming.

4. **The coaching leader** is focused on the developmental needs of each team member. He or she wants team members to get better and build personal strengths. This style doesn't work when team members are defiant or unwilling to learn or change behaviors. The team members must know that this leader knows what they are talking about to be effective. In this example, the leader does not need to do all the coaching. He or she can be a facilitator and ensure that the team receives the coaching it needs for the team to accomplish its mission or goals. Directing a team member to a seminar or training session to benefit the team might be most appropriate.

5. **The coercive leader** demands compliance. His words demand, "Do it my way!" This style works in a time of crisis and is short-lived. If used for a prolonged period, it can stifle team loyalty and creativity. At the first opportunity, a team member may bolt and leave for another team or organization. The team can self-destruct without the team leader fully knowing the reasons for the departure. Team members and team leaders need to get in front of differences before they become "irreconcilable differences," which might lead to a team breakup. You might hear such words as "he or she just wasn't a good fit" or "he just couldn't get his arms around what we were trying to accomplish." The leader must accept responsibility for his own actions.

6. **The democratic leader** builds consensus among team members and asks for feedback and opinions. This does not work if team members don't have the insight or

experience to render an effective opinion. When people feel their opinions are heard and that they are listened to, bonding, loyalty, high morale, and growth can be fostered in a positive way.

7. **The servant leader:** The phrase "servant leadership" was coined by Robert K. Greenleaf in "The Servant as Leader,"[7] an essay that he first published in 1970. In that essay, Greenleaf said:

> A servant-leader focuses primarily on the growth and well-being of people and the communities to which they belong. While traditional leadership generally involves the accumulation and exercise of power by one at the "top of the pyramid," servant leadership is different. The servant-leader shares power, puts the needs of others first and helps people develop and perform as highly as possible.

The point about leadership is that **a variety of styles can work at the right time and under the right set of circumstances**. What's important is to **recognize your leadership style** and maneuver in a variety of roles as circumstances may dictate. Leadership can shift among team members depending on the delegation of duties and responsibilities. This was especially true when we interviewed a trauma surgeon (later in Chapter 8, "Shock Trauma Surgery Teams: A Compare and Contrast View"). It's interesting how functional leadership can shift depending on the situation at hand.

Leadership Profile

What changes or action steps do you need to make to be a more effective leader on the team? Who can help you, or what can you do if you need help with the changes or action steps? Are you willing to make these changes? If not, why not?

Team Challenge

Each member of the team should describe their leadership profile and/or characteristics and discuss what changes they are willing to make to be a more effective leader. Use the styles discussed in this chapter as a guidepost.

NOTES

1. http://www.fastcompany.com/1838481/6-leadership-styles-and -when-you-should-use-them.
2. http://www.fastcompany.com/1838481/6-leadership-styles-and -when-you-should-use-them.
3. http://training.hr.ufl.edu/resources/LeadershipToolkit/tran scripts/SixEffectiveLeadershipStyles.pdf. (For more information, see http://intenseminimalism.com/2015/the-six-styles-of-leader ship/)
4. http://guides.wsj.com/management/developing-a-leadership -style/what-is-the-difference-between-management-and-leader ship/.
5. https://www.psychologytoday.com/blog/cutting-edge-leadership/ 200911/leadership-vs-management-what-s-the-difference.
6. http://guides.wsj.com/management/developing-a-leadership -style/what-is-the-difference-between-management-and-leader ship/.
7. The Greenleaf Center for Servant Leadership, www.greenleaf.org; revised edition, September 30, 2015.

5

Establishing a Vision, Mission Statement, Value Proposition, and Elevator Pitch

"A mission statement is not something you write overnight....But fundamentally, your mission statement becomes your constitution, the solid expression of your vision and values. It becomes the criterion by which you measure everything else in your life."

—Stephen Covey

This chapter is about confirming and/or creating the vision, mission statement, and value proposition for your team. This should also be discussed with each team member to determine if there is congruency of purpose. Team members want to have meaning and purpose in their lives. Vision and mission statements provide an inspirational purpose for your team and clients to rally around. They become part of the spirit of the team. We experience teams that operate without vision and purpose, and we find that they often act at cross purposes. The impact to the team occurs when no one can agree on a specific direction, how to handle clients, or establishing team agendas.

If you think about your vision as part of a dream and it is created without the involvement, feedback, or discussion of the other team members, then your vision or mission has been created in a vacuum. Team members might respond by saying, "That's your vision or mission, not mine! We do not agree on our purpose and values," thus giving rise to conflict or a breakup down the road.

Let's say I'm an outsider observing your team. I'm going to ask each team member three questions:

1. What is the vision of your team?
2. What is the mission statement of your team?
3. What is the team's value proposition?

Is the observer going to get a variety of responses like "I don't know," or "why is this important," or, perhaps, "we haven't really thought about it"?

Rationale: If you don't know where you're headed, how will you know when you arrive at your destination?

Let's discuss vision, mission, and value proposition with respect to teams.

A **vision statement** is the part of a team's message that ignites what your team is working toward. It's the dream, the end game. It also evokes a sense of achievement and fulfillment.

Here are a few examples:

> "To be nationally recognized for delivering an unrivaled combination of successful wealth management solutions and exceptional client service."

> "To empower my clients (and prospective clients) to reduce and eliminate their fears regarding their financial future."

> "We desire to be the preeminent financial advisor team in our market that provides a holistic approach to our clients and offers more than a commodity client experience."

> "We endeavor to know and understand your financial situation and provide you with only the highest-quality information, services, and products to help you reach your goals."

The purpose of your vision statement is to stretch boundaries and comfort zones and enable the people within the organization to have a sense of what could be.[1]

Your team's vision is a beacon of your hopes and desires of where your team is headed. It's the pathway. Without a vision, the team will not have all members aligned toward a common purpose. The act of pulling the team together to discuss the vision will draw your team together and begin the process of establishing a close bond with one another. This is a very important dynamic if the team's values are ever questioned. Allow your vision to be expansive. Remember, it's the destination you are moving toward.

Team Challenge

Discuss and draft your team's vision statement. Does it answer the following questions:

Does it inspire team members?
Does it create or strive for excellence in its purpose?
Is it ambitious?
Will it move the team from the present to the future?
Does it provide a clear direction?

Your Team's Vision Statement

_____
_____
_____
_____
_____
_____
_____

Mission Statement

Let's move to the subject of your team's mission statement. A team mission statement gets everyone on the same page and provides direction and clarity. This statement should describe the why and what you do as a team. Again, it helps to establish congruency on the team. It keeps team members from acting at cross purposes. We have seen teams flounder because there was not a clear direction or purpose. It seems as if everyone was moving in a different direction. This leads to frustration and is a critical failure point for any team. In crafting your mission statement, consider the core goals of your team.

What are some core elements for crafting your team's mission statement?

To develop your mission, here are some questions to ask:

- What do we do?
- For whom do we, do it?
- Why do we serve our clients in the way that we do?
- How do we serve our clients in the way that we do?
- Why are we in this industry?
- Why did we form our team?
- What image of our team do we want to convey?

Following are some sample mission statements to further explain the concept as you develop your statement:

Nike: To bring inspiration and innovation to every athlete in the world.

Starbucks: To inspire and nurture the human spirit – one person, one cup, and one neighborhood at a time.

Chevron: To be the global energy company most admired for its people, partnership, and performance.

Amazon: To be the most customer-centric company in the world, where people can find and discover anything they want to buy online.

Intel: Delight our customers, employees, and shareholders by relentlessly delivering the platform and technology advancements that become essential to the way we work and live.

eBay: Provide a global trading platform where practically anyone can trade practically anything.

Team Challenge

Write your aspirational and unifying team mission statement.

_____

_____

_____

_____

_____

_____

_____

_____

Value Proposition

Your team has now completed two very important elements of your business plan and strategy, namely, the vision statement and mission statement. It's important that the team members participate in the discussion, which creates team unity of purpose. Now let's discuss the **team's value proposition.** We have created a template in Figure 5.1 to provide some useful guidance to help you with this endeavor.

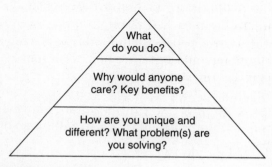

Figure 5.1 Value proposition.

A value proposition is a clear statement of the tangible results a customer gets from using your products or services. The more specific your value proposition is, the better. Write your value proposition, a statement that clearly defines what you do from the client's point of view, such as, "We are a financial resource to give you the confidence to make informed financial decisions."

Does your value proposition emotionally connect you with your client?

Team Challenge

Ask three or four of your clients how you provide value to them or what they perceive is the value that you are providing to them.

Start the conversation with this brief script: "Hi, Richard, thanks for meeting with me today. As part of our team's mission to provide you with the best possible service, I would like to ask you for some important feedback. I'd like you to think about the value we provide and tell me how you perceive the value and/or how you define the value you receive from our team." Take some notes and go back to your team and share the feedback. Determine if you need to make some adjustments to your value proposition. Hopefully, you will hear words or phrases like, "You're a trusted resource"; "you're my confidant on financial matters"; "you look out for the well-being of my family"; "your advice and guidance has helped us manage through the emotional ups and downs of volatile markets."

Once you answer the questions in Figure 5.1, your team will be on its way to crafting its value proposition. Asking clients what they experience when working with you will help solidify your value proposition.

Team Challenge

Craft your team's value proposition.

_____

_____

_____

_____

_____

_____

_____

_____

The 30-Second Elevator Pitch: A Supplement to Your Value Proposition

Sometimes you meet a person (prospect) for the first time and you need a concise explanation that captures the attention of a prospect. You want to leave a casual meeting with the prospect with them wanting more information. You might be at a museum gala, or special event gala, or receiving an introduction from someone you recently met at the country club. It's not always appropriate to provide a full explanation of your services. What you want to do is create an interest for the prospect to want to have a meeting with you. Then you are in a better position to provide more details about the services and capabilities of your team.

What do you offer or specialize in? The statement must have key benefits such as "help them make money, feel secure, and make them feel good." Author and entrepreneurial expert Chris O'Leary, COO, of Customer Innovations, Inc., a marketing consulting firm, is the author of _Elevator Pitch Essentials,_ published in 2008 by Limb Press LLC. He identified the following points to help with your elevator pitch[2]:

- **Concise:** Keep the pitch succinct and clear, with as few words as possible.
- **Clear:** The pitch should be easily understood by a layman, rather than filled with acronyms and industry terminology.
- **Compelling:** What problem does your business solve, and what can you do for your target audience?
- **Credible:** Spell out what makes you qualified to do what you do, without using buzzwords like *outside the box* or *synergy*. Using credibility-driven words like *certified* will help sell you.
- **Conceptual:** Keep your pitch broad; don't go into too many details.
- **Concrete:** The pitch should be tangible and easily grasped by your audience.
- **Customized:** Each target audience is different. The pitch should be tailored to the listeners.
- **Consistent:** No matter how many versions of your pitch you have, they should all convey the same basic message.
- **Conversational:** Start the conversation, and hook your target. Keep it casual, and don't try to close a deal in the pitch.

Introduction and Explanation of What You Do

Example: Hello, my name is Mary Jones. My team's practice is dedicated to being a trusted wealth management resource for affluent clients to build, manage, and preserve wealth. Our clients have found that my conservative strategies make them money, reduce risk, and help them feel secure.

The Problem(s) You Solve

You might say, "We help people meet their expectations and fulfill their dreams, hopes, and aspirations. The perfect client for our team is one who wants to play an active role in partnering with us to achieve their goals."

Open the Door and Invite Them In

If you know of someone who might be frustrated and not meeting their personal expectations for managing their wealth, it will be our pleasure to speak with them and offer a second opinion.

Team Challenge

Write a team-based 30-second elevator pitch.

_____

_____

_____

_____

_____

_____

_____

Again, we are trying to create a consistency of messaging by all team members.

Communication

As you can see from going through the team's effectiveness process, we are focused on making sure that individual team members do not operate in a vacuum or individual silo. Teams are most effective when straightforward communication takes place and everyone participates in meetings.

Communication – open communication – is where innovation and breakthrough results occur.

Rationale: How to conduct impactful meetings – agendas and key takeaways.

Let's discuss examples of types of meetings to conduct, their purpose, and what you hope to accomplish with your team.

In your meetings, make sure you criticize in private and provide praise in public. Criticism should be followed by two things that are being done right or correctly. You don't want to demotivate another team member. When someone is unduly criticized without any positive feedback, they walk away and often shut down for periods of hours and even days. They often go and share with 5 to 10 others in the office how you made them feel. The repercussions such as work stoppages can negatively impact productivity.

As you've learned from your Supernova training, each meeting should have an agenda. The agendas should be sent out in advance so that team members can come prepared to discuss the issues and topics. This leaves everyone feeling that they are prepared to make meaningful contributions. Listening and acknowledgment of another team member's point of view demonstrates that you are interested and that you care about their points of view and that they add value. I'm sure you have all been in unproductive meetings where there wasn't two-way communication. You probably left feeling very frustrated. Showing appreciation, recognition, and providing praise creates enthusiastic meetings and fosters communication.

Let's talk more about why this is so important. Here is an example of how things can get out of hand: So we have a team that is doing well in terms of productivity, but the junior member of the team decides to leave. This creates a little anxiety. The financial advisor also notices that the client associate is not looking him in the eye or speaking to him – only when spoken to. He has the sense that something is not right. Something is not working. So he goes in to talk to the manager and says, "I think I have a problem. I think there are some problems on the team. I don't quite know what they are or what to do about them, but it's going to impact my business if I don't get it fixed." Then he says, admittedly, "I've been on edge, I've been a little tense, and I think it spills over to the team members. I think I've been a little hard to work with. And before things really get out of hand, I need to do something about it."

With that manager now involved with the advisor's issue, the manager thinks, "I now have to coach this advisor to keep the whole thing from really blowing up." Sometimes it seems like everything is a crisis. Everything is urgent. Well, everything can't be urgent. But you must listen to your team members and get feedback. You must ask them how they are doing and what's on their minds. You must begin to run your team like it's a business, not just an assembly of people quickly put together with no alignment or strategy.

Given this situation with the team, the manager and the team leader of this team must go back and debrief the circumstances to figure out what went wrong, and how to fix this to avoid the entire team from blowing up. As we know, sometimes people don't say anything; they just vote with their feet. They just leave.

As we said, showing appreciation and recognition and providing praise creates enthusiastic meetings and fosters communication. It's so basic, but many advisors don't understand it, they don't do anything about it, and it's so important. This is not a criticism of advisors, but most are trained to be excellent advisors and not team leaders. Listening and acknowledging another team member's point of view is critical to the success of the team. It demonstrates that you care.

When a team leader comes in and is a benevolent dictator, and there's no feedback process for the team, emotions are held back and, ultimately, it leads to conflict. It becomes important to get people aligned. Get them on the same page. Then have your team meeting.

Prior to a team meeting, ask the participants if there is an important item that they would like to place on the agenda. In our experience, team meetings should be specific. If there are too many topics on the agenda, the likelihood of accomplishing the goals for the session are in doubt. Teams must stick to agendas, and time limits must be adhered to. When meetings continuously run over, members become disenchanted and don't look forward to attending. Help to make the meeting fun and enjoyable.

The Short Team Huddle – 10 Minutes in Length

This meeting should take place first thing in the morning. All team members should gather around one desk and discuss the agenda for the day with the team. Any issues or concerns should be brought up during this session. This should be reserved for very urgent matters the team is focused on. Short huddles reduce time spent in lengthy meetings.

Team Performance Review (30 Minutes)

Teams should discuss the game board,[3] which is a list of specific and measurable team goals. Did the team achieve its goals for client contact, client acquisition, planning, revenue, prospect meetings, and referrals for the week? Teams will want to measure and apply weekly progress checks on performance. This gives the team the opportunity to adjust or create midcourse corrections right away. Think about it this way. At the end of the month, one twelfth of the year has passed. By the time adjustments or corrections are made, perhaps two more weeks have passed. The team loses traction and valuable time. If the team waits for quarter-end to adjust, 25% of the year has passed.

Team Strategy Retreat (One Half-day Away from the Office)

This is a half-day meeting away from the office. The team creates a formal agenda with everyone providing input to the topics. Each member will make a report or discuss their activities. The team's overall strategy and business plan are discussed. Time should be allocated on the agenda for brainstorming or idea sharing. The team can discuss its goals, vision, strengths, opportunities, and action plan. This is where the team does the "deep dive" on its plans. A "deep dive" exercise involves more than a quick fix to a client's problems. It involves taking a closer examination and holistic view and analysis of a number of factors impacting a client's planning and investment strategies. If there are other strategic partners relevant to the team's success, you might want to invite them to a portion of your meeting. There's a lot of flexibility for the team to focus on its individual needs and strategy development.

Team Training Meetings

There are times when the team must focus on its specific training needs. These sessions can focus on product or service education, changes in the regulatory environment, compliance, or specific topics that relate to niche markets and team development. A team might participate in webinars, podcasts, or conference calls for this development or participate in off-site training and seminars. The point here is that team members are "knowledge workers" and must be committed to a lifelong learning process. The point about meetings is to make them relevant, focused, and agenda specific. Agenda items that aren't urgent get tabled for the next session.

Some of your meetings will be strategic in nature. You will want to discuss the team's key initiatives, progress on tasks, timing, and the responsible person who leads the initiative. You will want to evaluate, measure, and discuss progress toward goals, as shown in Table 5.1.

Some of your plans or goals might be more tactical such as goals for planning and plan implementation. Reference the game board in your Supernova manual. The idea is to measure

Table 5.1 Action plan initiative: Client meetings.

Task	Timing	Responsibility	Target date for completion
Estate planning seminar	Start 08/15	Joe & insurance specialists	08/31
Client appreciation reception	Start 09/08	Mary	10/02

Table 5.2   Game board.

Activity	Goal	Actual	Week ending
Financial plans	4	3	07/27
Plans implemented	5	2	
New households	3	3	
New assets	1 million	2 million	
Referrals received	5	7	
Client appointments	10	9	
Prospect appointments	5	4	

the team's performance versus goals. There is obviously a host of objectives that you want to measure that impact team productivity. Table 5.2 lists a few items to think about.

The team should meet once per week and discuss the activities that are being measured in accordance with goals versus actual performance. The communication between team members should be an open discussion about performance, measurement, improvements, and what team members are doing well and what items or tasks need more attention. Praise should be given for exceeding expectations. The team should discuss barriers to success and key failure points. Team members should be given responsibility and ownership for key measures or drivers for team performance. Always end your meeting[4] on a positive note. Open discussions in team meetings will go a long way to establish **trust** among each team member.

Practice, Drill, and Rehearse

Preparing for a major client or prospect meeting is like a surgery team preparing for a major surgery, a sports team preparing for game day, or a military special operations team preparing for a mission. You discuss as much information that you have with each other about the client or prospect. Assuming you've done your homework and have conducted an extensive profile, you want to use this time to organize for action. Which team member will lead the discussion and agenda? What role(s) will each team member play in the meeting and presentation?

What is the order of communication with the client/prospect? How will questions be handled? Who will close the business or ask the client/prospect for a commitment to do business? Will handouts be required? Who will bring them? We suggest that the team walk through and visualize the entire meeting. This practice, drill, and rehearsal will ensure that the team is well prepared for that important meeting.

After the Client/Prospect Meeting Is Over

Once the client meeting is over, who will be responsible for sending out a brief executive summary of what was discussed, what was agreed to, and any commitments that were made during the meeting? Also, any follow-up items such as the providing of materials and copies of insurance policies for review should be indicated in the executive summary. There are items that the team needs to follow up on and items the client needs to follow up on as well. This summary is a confirmation of what both parties have committed to do. Use the executive summary for prospect meetings as well. Immediately following the meeting, send out an executive summary, no more than two paragraphs in length via e-mail. In the e-mail, summarize the discussion, what you both agreed on, concerns that will be addressed, and priorities that came up during the conversation. You will also identify the next steps in the relationship and topics or information gathering needed to establish a relationship with you. This is a presumptive close. Bring the account opening documents to the next meeting and say, "I would like to get started working with you right away." Why procrastinate any further?

The executive summary is a reminder for both parties that there are open action items for further discussion at an appointed time. This should be sent out within 24 hours of the meeting. The executive summary is important because it gives the conversation focus and can create a sense of urgency on the part of the prospect/client to take action. It's the beginning of establishing your value and your professionalism for the new client. It's part of the client experience process. Use this as a tool to bring more prospects across the finish line and increase or add to the number of client relationships.

The executive summary also provides a record of the discussion from a compliance perspective. Remember, you must be a leader in helping to direct the prospect to a course of action that is in their best interest. Once your team's vision, mission statement, and value proposition is created, don't tuck it away in a desk drawer never to be seen or referenced again. Take the time to remind the team members what everyone is working toward – a common vision. This is your team's aspirational message.

> ### Team Challenge
>
> Establish a team meeting with an agenda on a topic of your choice. Have all participants evaluate the meeting in terms of what worked well and areas for improvement.

NOTES

1. http://www.makeadentleadership.com/developing-a-team -vision-statement.htm.
2. http://www.businessnewsdaily.com/3937-elevator-pitch.html.
3. Robert D. Knapp, *The Supernova Advisor: Crossing the Invisible Bridge to Exceptional Client Service and Consistent Growth* (Hoboken, NJ: John Wiley & Sons, 2008).
4. http://www.inc.com/peter-economy/5-steps-to-great-meetings .html.

Operationalizing the Five Star Model

"From a young age, I learned to focus on the things I was good at and delegate to others what I was not good at. That's how Virgin is run. Fantastic people throughout the Virgin Group run our businesses, allowing me to think creatively and strategically."

—Richard Branson

The **Five Star Model** is the delegation of duties and responsibilities for each team member. While the model has its structure, you need to be flexible, call an audible (divert from planned structure as in a football play) at times, and delegate a task to the team member most capable of getting a specific task or tasks done. The important takeaway regarding the Five Star Model is that it identifies leadership responsibilities for the team and holds a team member accountable for specific functions on the team. Each star represents a significant responsibility that a team member has accountability to lead.

It is difficult to move the team forward without first deciding on defining key roles and the overall delegation of duties and responsibilities. In small vertical teams with one senior producer, one junior producer, and one client associate, certain roles will be duplicated. Both advisors might be responsible for planning, for example. We have found that teams work best when every member of the team has a role in client-facing activities and new client development.

The **first star** would be planning to ensure that every client has a financial plan. He or she is like a forensic scientist understanding what the client really wants, not just what they say they want. The vice president (our designation) sets standards, goals, and follow-up guidelines for the team.

The **second star** deals with planning implementation, which is basically overseeing the investment process. This vice president is responsible to make sure all parts of the plan are implemented consistently for every client. This typically includes mortgages, insurance, tax planning, long-term care, and other products in addition to investments. The plan identifies some specific concepts and ideas that the client should implement, and the team member responsible for implementation will make sure that these concepts are followed through.

The **third star** represents brand and service – and the service model relates to the client experience. This vice president is responsible for brand consistency through monitoring segmentation, rapid response to client issues, overseeing the scheduling of 12-4-2 client appointments, and compliance issues. The scheduling of 12-4-2 refers to monthly client contact with eight monthly updates and four quarterly reviews, of which two are in person and two are phone reviews. Compliance is a natural addition as the organizational duties provide a natural high-compliance posture. Regular client contact, rapid response to problems, networking opportunities in writing, and executive summaries of agreed-on action (follow-up executive summaries, e-mails) all eliminate compliance issues. Keeping track of all the correspondence and putting it into a customer relationship management (CRM) system or permanent client record will give you added insurance in case of a compliance issue.

Next is the **fourth star,** vice president of marketing, who is responsible for overseeing the acquisition strategy of the team (90/6/4/2/2/1 + VIPSA). This vice president sets the standards strategies and goals for the team and then follows up on the set guidelines. The Supernova Acquisition Strategy includes a 90-day free look for prospects, six Centers of Influence for each member of the team, a four-member Mastermind Group for each member of the team, two niches per advisor, volunteering on two nonprofit boards, a social media strategy (includes website, LinkedIn, etc.), and VIPSA. VIPSA refers to asking clients for introductions to prospects. VIPSA is an acronym. The V refers to asking clients what they *value* from the client experience they receive from you. The I refers to asking clients what is *important* to them. The P is seeking *permission* to brainstorm with the client potential prospects that can be personally introduced to you. The S refers to a *suggestion* as to how an introduction to the prospect might take place or simply asking the client how do you *suggest* I meet him or her? The A in this model refers to *advice*. Asking the client for their *advice* as to how you might best connect with a potential prospect makes a client feel valued and that the clients opinion matters.

The **fifth star** focuses on leadership. This vice president is responsible for developing and maintaining a productive environment through team confidence, team skills, team knowledge, and team accountability. This vice president helps the team release its inner potential by choosing growth over fear, and he or she will build time into the schedule for monthly meetings with individual members of the team, create a folder for each member as if they were a client, and work with them to develop their skills based on the goals that were established.

The person selected should be a team member who helps to drive that accountability: Someone who is really good at inspiring team members to take action. This person is not necessarily what we call a "manager." We look at these functions as being leadership functions, not management. So the team gets together and the members decide on who that person is going to be. They look at the skills and experience to determine where these responsibilities should lie.

It could possibly be a challenge if there is a team where no one wants to take a leadership role: "It's not my job, man!" Dodging responsibility and accountability is a team dysfunction that must be addressed.

Avoid the Leaderless Team

There are plenty of team activities to go around, but the person who is the most capable for the role of leader must be accountable for moving the team toward accomplishing its strategic plan. Now, that doesn't mean that each team member does not share leadership responsibilities. It does mean, however, that there is one person who will be accountable for making sure that everything runs smoothly. There may be a specific task, for example, in marketing, where two people may take the lead in putting together the seminar for the team. That doesn't necessarily mean that the team leader is going to execute on that task.

In some cases, there may be multiple roles, especially if it's a small vertically integrated team. There might be a senior advisor, a junior advisor, and a client associate. Now if these folks are vice presidents who are assigned to each of these key areas – the five stars – one may be responsible for planning for the team and may also carry on some specific roles in marketing and sales. Another team member will take on the leadership role and have some service oversight for the team. The client associate may take on the entire team's administrative scheduling and overall responsibility for the client experience and team service model.

In reference to the implementation of a client financial plan, for example, you will find that there are investment ideas and concepts to be discussed. Perhaps managed solutions, portfolio management and rebalancing, the liability side of the client's balance sheet, lending, mortgages, credit – all those initiatives are a result of what may be outcomes of the plan.

You might ask, how can everything get done, how can it all be coordinated, and how can it all be overseen by one person who's accountable? As previously discussed, the sole practitioner model has limitations in fulfilling the client experience. The sole practitioner advisor is, for the most part, a "jack-of-all-trades." He or she is responsible for all the activities associated with managing the business. Everything from prospecting to client acquisition, research, financial planning, investment strategies and selection, clients needing portfolio reviews – these are all the responsibilities of a sole practitioner advisor. While this list is not in any way exhaustive, we are sure you understand our point. This model is hard to scale while delivering a service model that is exceptional. Elements of client service, and especially client-facing activities, begin to suffer. Thus, we see client turnover and a business that has flat-lined in terms of growth. In many cases, the practice has stalled and experiences diminished returns relative to revenue growth.

We have seen a real evolution over the years because the team business models have evolved since the 1970s. The business model was simple. We were stockbrokers, buying and selling stocks. That was pretty much it. Then the business evolved and stockbrokers were called account executives, which led to descriptions such as financial consultants and, currently, financial advisors. The competitive landscape started to change. Firms began to create more products and services to secure client relationships. Then, all these products and services started to multiply – more than 150 in many firms. We experienced this gray area, in terms of what's a brokerage firm, what's a bank, and what's an insurance company? What that meant was that the individual sole practitioner came into the business thinking the business model was fixed and established. We weren't quite prepared for the rapid pace of change going on in the industry. Our mind-set and training at the time was focused on selling and transactions. The evolution came with the introduction of financial planning capabilities. It would set the stage for using products to solve specific client problems. This was a difficult transition for many of our peers and the industry as a whole. It would take a considerable amount of time to make that transformation.

An evolution in the business began to take place, which resulted in the advisor firm's business model changing at a rapid pace. As a result, the structure of the advisor's business model had to evolve as well into a team-based model. This team model continues to evolve into a more collaborative business model. The advisor team collaborates with de-facto team members consisting of a firm's specialists that support the team, and partnering with the client's other advisors. They may be an attorney, certified public accountant (CPA), insurance agent, and lender if these services are not provided directly by the advisor's team of specialists. This is the future dynamic as we see it. Enabling this collaborative model to work effectively is a team challenge for many reasons. There are enormous sensitivities around who owns the client relationship and how revenues should be shared across functions, departments, or other contributing silo businesses. This is a dynamic tension that must be resolved to the overall satisfaction of the team members.

It can be frustrating for the advisor at times, who may think, "How can I get all this work [research, portfolio management, rebalancing, account reviews, financial planning, investment strategies, and client acquisition] done with the amount of time I have available?" What we're hearing is that there's no time to do the work and their personal lives suffer. It impacts time for vacations, time to go to a child's sporting event, health and fitness, and a host of other issues leading to career dissatisfaction and frustration. Not to mention shortfalls in serving the needs of the clients.

What can be done to help? There are technology-driven applications designed to simplify some of these issues for clients. If the advisor isn't truly in the advice guidance business and doing the "deep dive," the old way of doing business gives way to competitive threats, that is, technology disruptors and other advisory organizations. These disruptors evolve their roles and business models, and the result creates an intense competitive environment.

But what is the main difference between the sole practitioner model versus the team? The team can provide several services and capabilities and make the kind of client-facing or customer contact that a sole practitioner is unable to do. If you specialize as a sole practitioner, you're going to concede potential business opportunities due to your bandwidth. Also, the potential for other entities, disruptors, and advisors may gain access to your clients and data via positioning other products or services. This can lead to your primary services being disrupted. Who wants to risk client relationships that take considerable time and effort to develop? Teams can leverage hybrid models characterized by both personal service via the advisor and digital capabilities to achieve scale.

However, there's the advisor under the insurance company umbrella who comes in through the back door and says, "Wow, your estate is at a level where we've got to provide protection for you and your family," and they come in and get inventory of all the assets, where they're domiciled, and then begin to chip away at some of the services that you're providing. It's a risk and it renders your business model obsolete. That's the real battlefront in the industry right now.

Who Is Going to Gain Competitive Advantage and Increase the Share of the Client's Wallet?

What we're finding now is that many teams have expanded to $250 million, $500 million, $1 billion, and more in assets. For all intents and purposes, these are real businesses. We describe them as "intrapreneurs" inside the broader bank, brokerage, or insurance company businesses. The key element about all of this is now the teams can provide more than a commodity client experience, and teams will have limits on the number of household relationships that can effectively be managed. If it's done right, the team can acquire more revenue per household – by doing a "deeper dive" or providing a holistic approach to the client relationship.

Clients will know you are giving them a level of service they won't be able to get elsewhere and are more likely to give your team more assets to manage. We often refer to this concept as "sticky assets," or assets less likely to leave the advisor relationship. But remember, advisors must earn the right to acquire all of a client's assets no matter what the choice of business model. There is a tension emerging between the personal advice of an advisor and technology-driven advice channels.

Tools to Help Operationalize: Technology, Training, and the Human Touch

If you're going to operationalize the team, it must be managed under a common schedule that every team member can view and, of course, see each team member's activities. When members schedule appointments, client meetings, and team meetings, it all goes into a central calendar capability. There are tools available for teams to do that effectively and efficiently, CRM tools that integrate e-mail with calendars and client contact systems.

We're big believers in giving a client a folder that memorializes discussions. If a client has an idea they think warrants a discussion, and it's in between meetings, they could simply write it down in their folder: "I want to discuss something with my advisor that I read about," or "I want to talk to my advisor about the potential for refinancing my mortgage." We always stress that the first agenda that is discussed is the client agenda. When a client call is scheduled, the client simply goes into their folder and recalls previous conversations and notes items for discussion with their advisor. Why a folder? It is available quickly and is readily accessible.

Next, you go through the items that you've identified in the calendar, and at the end of that discussion you send out an executive summary, which highlights what was discussed, what was agreed to, and what commitments that were made. The client will have a copy of the summary to put in his folder and you will have a copy that you will keep in your folder. It also reminds the client of the next scheduled call. When it's time for the call/appointment, the advisor pulls the client folder and has a recap of the previous conversation with the client prior to discussing the new business agenda. The first agenda discussed is always the client's agenda. Some advisors store this information with various cloud-based solutions, such as Box. Software applications, such as the box.com, enable cloud file storage and provide access to the end user for those that trend toward paperless activities. Of course, you need to determine what your firm and what your compliance department allows.

Important reminder: Whenever you use technology in client facing, you must understand sometimes it can be impersonal. At times, your strategic advantage is the "personal touch" you're able to provide. It's important to balance how you use your technology and think about the importance of a "personal touch" that you can give to clients. It might be a handwritten note of thanks, as opposed to an e-mail. The number of e-mails that clients are getting is overwhelming! What you want to be careful of is letting the volume of e-mails get to a point where clients are just ignoring them. If you decide to offer a "personal touch," it might provide better responses. It's the personal relationship and that personal touch that seems to resonate with the clients.

In terms of technology, perhaps one or more team members don't have the functional expertise to use certain technology tools. Then you must think about how they're going to acquire it and how they're going to get trained on the tools or applications. If your client associate needs to get up to speed on technology that your team needs to use, you must be willing to send that person to a one- or two-day training session. Consider that all knowledge workers need training for personal growth and development. They will make better contributions to the team.

Remember, the purpose of the Five Star Model is to divide the team responsibilities into categories so nothing falls through the cracks. If you're not good at some of these delegated responsibilities, you must develop your skill set to improve your use of certain tools, or bring on a team member who might be better at a technology application that you do not fully understand. If there's an expertise that the team doesn't have, they may have to either partner with another advisor and/or another team that has a specific level of proficiency that provides leverage for your team.

We frequently encounter teams that have expanded to the point of having too many client relationships that create unmanageable scenarios. There is not enough available time to service additional clients, or the best clients are underserved due to time constraints. One team we coached was stuck on the scheduling of client calls and appointments. There didn't seem to be enough hours in the day to reach their clients in a consistent manner and they were becoming overwhelmed with the number of households and relationships they managed. They asked us for help during one of their sessions. We determined this was about two things: The lack of consistent and scheduled segmentation and delegation of duties and responsibilities. Teams segment once to get organized then over a period of time they start taking on more and more client relationships but don't keep up with the segmenting. One of the keys to segmenting is setting your maximum number of clients and minimum number of assets you will accept and updating it regularly. This team was bringing on 40 to 60 new relationships a year and the team was reluctant to reassign them to another advisor in the office due to the additional revenues they were generating. They were really concerned that without adding more staff, they couldn't deliver the type of service they felt they should be providing. The team members were very concerned about the demands of a robust clientele and maintaining the growth and client service.

The challenge for this team was they must continuously determine who they can really work with and how many relationships they can manage to effectuate the service model. Everyone has their responsibilities for client acquisition on the team, but the team also must take responsibility for making sure that clients are directed to the appropriate channel. This channel might be a client service center. For others, delegating clients to another advisor or advisor team. Teams must continuously manage their capacity in terms of the number of clients/households. They must review asset size and revenue per relationship and make the tough decision as to what clients to keep.

And let's not forget about the related relationships that are smaller in asset size but might be related to a primary client relationship. We have coined those relationships "butlers." They are usually the children of your best clients, but they could also be the friend of a family member or a relative. What happens in those cases is that the advisor has quarterly meetings with them instead of monthly meetings, with one of the appointments being in person for a review. Three of those individuals is equal to one client. You must balance how many of the smaller relationships you are willing to take on without diminishing the team performance and capability to service your primary client relationships. Make sure the team doesn't suffer a diminished return and/or get so consumed with handling the smaller relationships at the expense of your wealthier clients. Again, it's keeping a balance and treating all clients fairly.

Team Challenge

Schedule a team meeting and review the delegation of duties and responsibilities using the Five Star Model. Ask each team member if there are any gaps on the team that need to be addressed.

7

Team Collaboration

"Alone we can do so little; together we can do so much."
—Helen Keller

$\mathbf{T}$eams that don't have certain capabilities to meet the needs of clients will need to partner or collaborate with another advisor either within your office or outside the office. It's this internal and external collaboration that takes the team and/or partnering to a new level. It's the collective wisdom that you bring to bear on a client relationship that can enable your team to be hypercompetitive and really provide differentiated expertise and a competitive advantage. (See the team collaborative model diagram in Figure 7.1.)

The advisor team is the centerpiece for coordinating both internal collaborative relationships and external collaborative relationships. We classify these relationships as your expanded team members. Let's describe these relationships as we have arrows in the diagram that emanate from the core, which is the advisor team.

The **branch manager** is sometimes an underutilized expanded team member. The branch manager can help you navigate the firm and provide key talent resources for significant client relationships you are trying to attract to the firm. The manager should be your **business strategist** and help provide business planning and strategy guidance similar to the way in which the advisor provides guidance to his/her clients. Sometimes, inviting a manager to a significant client/prospect appointment might be enough to bring in more assets to your team and firm. The client sees that management stands behind the team and supports the client's best interests. The manager

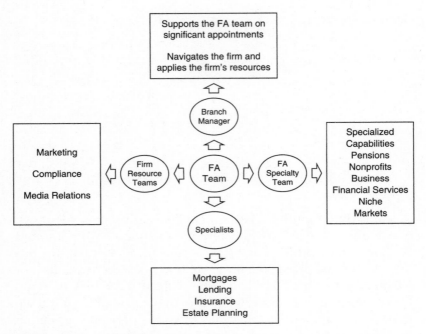

Figure 7.1   Collaborative team model.

can be useful for the more significant relationships you are trying to close.

The **advisor specialty team** may have expertise and capabilities that don't exist on your team. For example, this team may have capabilities in doing business with endowments and nonprofits that you don't have on your team. You would partner with this team and leverage its expertise. It's this multidisciplinary approach that can bring the most appropriate skill sets to the client relationship. As the complexity of the wealth management business continues to evolve, it becomes increasingly more challenging to have all the necessary skills that reside on one team. Your team would work out a split/fee-sharing arrangement and share revenues generated from closed business for a period of time. We recommend teams memorialize this arrangement in writing. When you consider the competitive nature of the wealth management business, this type of team collaboration is hard to disrupt.

Collaboration and Team Growth

Many financial advisor teams develop clients that share common threads. They may forge relationships with small business owners, business executives, attorneys, and physicians. Over time, they begin to understand the specialized needs of these clients and can develop specialty niche markets. Niche marketing is defined as reaching a subset of a broader market. Many advisors choose not to specialize in niche markets because they can be limiting in terms of scalability, meaning that there are not enough clients in a market to successfully grow a practice.

In Florida, for example, it would be hard to ignore the retiree market as a specialized niche. In the Silicon Valley in California, it would be hard to ignore the entrepreneurial market in technology. A subset of this market might be to fully understand Rule 144 sales of securities and how to accommodate the needs of executives who receive restricted stock and stock options as part of their compensation package. If you don't have expertise in accommodating the needs of this customer base, it might be important to collaborate with a team that fully understands this capability.

Specialists and specialty teams hone their skills over a period of years, and it might be important to bring this specialty skill set to the client or prospect relationship. It's the unique capability that the specialist team brings to the table that can enhance your client relationship. Yes, you must create a fee-sharing relationship that considers the other team's time spent on the relationship through the initial presentation, the close of business, and follow-up after specific strategies have been implemented. Unfair splits on revenue between teams is a nonstarter for the relationship.

If a lawyer can bring in a forensic accountant on a legal case or a trauma surgeon can bring in an orthopedic surgeon on a high-profile trauma case, then financial advisors can bring in an expert or specialist team to solve a problem for an important client relationship. It has been our experience that many financial advisors and teams simply concede the business or try to maneuver in unfamiliar territory. As a result, they either don't deliver the best client experience or deliver an experience that would lead to more business and referrals.

One of the key reasons that collaboration or partnering is a challenge is that the culture of many firms doesn't necessarily reward sharing arrangements, or collaboration hasn't been institutionalized among teams or business units. Also, the absence of trust between teams is a factor when you have another team intercede on an important client relationship. Firms will need to be supportive in overcoming the issue of trust in optimizing the best solutions for the client.

Team leadership in complex client cases becomes more functional and is based on the situation at hand. Leadership might rotate between the specialist and the key person in charge of the client relationship. In our experience, we have seen this work superbly well; however, it is not as widespread as it could potentially become.

Let's say your team has just received a lead from a client who sits on the board of a major hospital. The hospital has put out a request for proposal (RFP) for a $100 million endowment. Your team has no experience in this area. What do you do? Rather than move into uncharted territory, you identify a team outside of your office that has years of experience in this very area. They know exactly what to do and how to respond. In fact, they have worked with other advisor teams before and understand the sensitivities around compensation splits, relationship management, and the best way to respond to the RFP. You decide to select this experienced team; however, you stay involved in the process, which is critical to the relationship.

There are some terrific team benefits to be gained through collaboration.

- Collaboration raises your level of competency in the eyes of the client. This leads to client retention, more assets, and can potentially lead to referrals.
- Provides an additional avenue of revenue that may not have been previously available to the team. Solving complex problems and opening new avenues for growth can lead to more assets which is a key driver of business growth.

- It's a client first strategy and helps with client retention. Team values require that you put the needs of the client above your own needs. This improves your reputation in the markets you serve.
- The competitive nature of the business allows collaboration to provide a wider access to capabilities in support of the client. The industry experiences price compression and technology disruption. Collaboration is your disruptive threat.
- This leverage can accelerate team growth due to greater client penetration. The Force Multiplier Effect and impact is all about serving the needs of your clients.
- Using technology, you can create the equivalent of the 911 call of virtual expertise. Whether you use the phone, "GoToMeeting" communication, or Skype to have a face-to-face meeting, working virtually can have its advantages when a partnering team is domiciled outside of your market area.

One such specialty team we helped to form more than a decade ago consisted of three team members. They came together with the thought that their practice could evolve to include philanthropic services, nonprofits, and endowments. The team has received special accreditation and is accredited by their firm's Global Institutional Consulting (GIC), a group of approximately 80 consultants. The team has a host of certifications and accreditations that define their areas of expertise. They also have two client associates that complement the team business.

It bears repeating: You partner with a specialty team because they have a level of expertise and competency that doesn't reside on your team. If you have worked in the for-profit and nonprofit sectors, you know they are quite different; each has its own culture, vernacular, and business practices. Many well-meaning advisors approach nonprofit and charitable organizations seeking to partner with them in their fundraising efforts. Some are successful, while others are not.

To properly execute business in this sector you need to have received some training in several key areas, primarily in creating investment policy statements and planned giving concepts, and understanding tax and legal implications involved in this niche market. This is a complicated area that may not be in your team's "wheelhouse of expertise."

Finally, you need to understand the backgrounds and motivations of the board members. Creating a collaborating arrangement with a team that is experienced in this niche market is the way to go. Bringing a team with this niche specialization to an appointment can only enhance your creditability in the eyes of the client or prospect.

The use of **specialists** in mortgages, estate planning, long-term care, and lending are used to extend specific expertise to the client. The specialist may come with you to an important meeting with a client or can be available telephonically or virtually. External vendors also fall under this category and can provide resources and resource people to help with client acquisition. We have found that these specialists' relationships work best when there is a clear, confident relationship between the specialist and the advisor team. Lawyers bring in expert witnesses and surgeons bring in experts on complex surgeries. It shouldn't be out of the ordinary for an advisor team to provide resource people for important client meetings or complex issues. Again, this could be a team's competitive advantage or differentiating factor in gaining or retaining important client relationships. It's important that teams embrace these specialists as partners and not outsiders.

The **firm's resource teams** may be in a product or a marketing area, compliance as well as media relations, as an example. This resource can be helpful as you work on bringing significant relationships into the firm and go after niche markets. Again, using technology and videoconferencing, when appropriate, to connect these experts and resource people to clients can make the difference between winning a meaningful relationship, retaining a relationship, and providing the best service. It can be a constant struggle to understand where some of these resources reside in the firm; however, it can create the Force Multiplier Effect and have a positive impact on a client relationship.

Teams can create **virtual teaming** situations with all the above examples to bring collective wisdom and expertise when needed to grow and improve client relationships. Virtual teams are increasingly common. Members of a team may rarely meet in person. They collaborate from various parts of the country through telephone calls, e-mail, file-sharing technology, and face-to-face capabilities such as GoToMeeting and other online meeting methods.

We worked with a two-person financial advisor (FA) team that was split between Atlanta and Dallas. They spoke by phone every day, and their one client service associate was in Atlanta scheduling appointments for both. It worked for them because they communicated so often. They could accelerate their growth by working both markets, and when there was a larger client ($10 million or more), they would both meet with them.

Getting people to work together for a common purpose is easier said than done. We have experienced that when teams come together in a collaborative way and utilize the collective wisdom of other team members within the organization, "magic" can happen. Fostering cooperation does require a cultural change. Perhaps some of the barriers to cooperation are firmly entrenched in one part of the organization not trusting another part of the organization, or compensation and fee-sharing arrangements are not clear or become an impediment to collaboration. Some of the examples we have seen in silos where there is separation between functional groups operating under separate compensation arrangements. Usually, there may not be specific compensation strategies between groups that reward cooperation. Cultural differences when groups are competing for the same client can also lead to the avoidance of cooperation. The needs of the client must come first despite these impediments that impact the client experience.

Collaboration with Clients' Other Advisors

There are clients that prefer relationships with their personal banker, insurance agent, estate planning attorney, and certified public accountant. Rather than try to break an emotional bond that the client has established with these professionals, develop a strategy to meet with them and collaborate. Then use them to refer to other clients. We call that the Enthusiastically Endorsed List. When these key relationships exist, advisor teams should welcome the opportunity to collaborate and act in the best interest of the client. If the relationships can grow and prosper, they could potentially become a strong referral source to grow a team's client base. In our experience, having the client make a personal introduction over coffee or lunch leads to developing a strong relationship. Always ask first if the client can enthusiastically endorse the external advisor. If not, there may be an opportunity for you to provide a referral of someone you feel more comfortable recommending to the client – usually someone who has been enthusiastically endorsed by other clients.

Compensation systems that reward teamwork and cooperation have the potential to outperform those organizations where collaboration is not encouraged. Not all team-based metrics should be based entirely on a revenue model. Teams can prosper when reviewing collaboration and its impact on team productivity. Teams should evaluate all their team-based activities that contribute to performance and make sure that team members and those individuals that support the team are rewarded. Rewards, of course, can be monetary and nonmonetary. Don't wait until the end of the year to let a team member know that the work they are doing is appreciated. At times, and after team members have been working close together, members may feel underappreciated or taken for granted. Sometimes a day off, tickets to a play or sporting event, or dinner for two can go a long way in making a team member feel valued and appreciated.

Team Challenge

Identify how your team members are rewarded and shown appreciation.

The Force Multiplier Effect

Teams must collaborate among themselves to gain leverage and improve productivity. An area of struggle for many teams is the integration of individual books of business or clients. One way to accomplish this integration is to define a primary relationship manager, a secondary relationship manager, and – in the case of three producers – a tertiary relationship manager. Each team member works as the primary relationship manager for a specific number of households and, when not available, steps into the role of secondary relationship manager and pulls the client file folder (hard copy or electronic) and supports the client when the primary relationship manager is out of the office or on vacation, for example.

If teams can improve and leverage the collaborative team model, then it would be the equivalent of creating a **force multiplier,** a capability that, when added to and employed by a team, significantly increases the productivity potential of that team and enhances the probability of a successful mission accomplishment. In other words, a small and agile team that can carry a powerful punch! The definition comes from the military and is used to describe the multiplier effect and factor for combat advantage when using people, technology, and capable assets with a small unit. Utilizing these assets can enable a small unit to act as a large, formidable force.

> In the [Navy] SEALs [Special Operations Unit], our force multiplier came in both internal and external forms depending on the mission. Externally, our force multipliers were close air support, unmanned aerial vehicles providing intelligence, surveillance and reconnaissance of a known target (area). Internally, it was the skill and will of each team member, the team's ability to work together, and the speed at which we could learn, move and adapt – as individuals and as a team – to change and uncertainty.[1]

A three-person team in a collaborative effort can have the multiplier impact of more than double its size and capabilities if managed appropriately. If done right, teams could contribute significantly more in organic growth for the firms that employ them. Creating cooperative and collaborative organizations is the key to success. In our experience, this works best when visions, missions, and compensation systems are all strategically aligned and act in the best interest of the client. When teams act with precision, every team member understands their role, and everyone is aligned and focused on the mission, breakthroughs happen. Effective collaboration is a real game changer for teams to experience breakout growth.

We believe that teams can learn through the observations of other professional teams. A former naval fighter pilot and member of the prestigious naval flight demonstration team, the Blue Angels, was asked about his team experience. This is an example of the pursuit of excellence and continuous training, collaboration, trust, precision, and execution. He shared the following story with us.

A Team Perspective from a Naval Aviator

I smartly climbed into the cockpit of my F/A-18 Hornet. Unlike my previous squadron, I did not conduct a preflight inspection of my aircraft. That was done by my crew chief. I had total confidence that our ground crew had performed their responsibilities to perfection. I was willing to bet my life on it. They were part of our overall team. I had complete confidence that the aircraft I was mounting was completely safe for flight.

As I climbed into the seat of the aircraft, my crew chief helped me strap in and offered a final handshake before stepping off the airplane. One final check of all switches and now we await the signal to close the canopy, fire up the auxiliary power unit, and then bring the engines to life.

Takeoff checks in the chocks and a taxi to the runway. The flight leader gives his orders in a smooth and melodic manner. "Smoke on, off brakes now, burners ready now!!" Four F/A-18 Hornets leap up slightly as the brakes are released. Each aircraft slides into flight as the physics of thrust and lift take over. The slot pilot calls for the gear; each of us reaches for the knob without looking down. The gear is up; we push the noses forward on the flight leader's command, to accelerate even more as we begin our first maneuver. I'm now "flying paint" on the flight leader's aircraft, a place that will occupy my sight for the next 40 minutes. It is a combination of blue and gold, a missile rail or a wing that will be between 18 and 36 inches away from me at most times. The flight leader calls "up we go," and I gently pull back on the stick, matching my distance and bearing on the lead aircraft. Our first maneuver has begun.

As a member of the Navy's Flight Demonstration Squadron, the Blue Angels, each maneuver is practiced in the pursuit of perfection. Countless hours are spent on the ground and in the air going through each maneuver and all the paces. Each member of the team knows exactly what to do and when to execute.

No detail is left undone. From the flight suit to the spit-shined boots to the walk down, everything is briefed, practiced, and reviewed. We are a team and we execute as a team. Individuality is the biggest threat to team harmony and flight safety. Prima donnas and egomaniacs are quickly vetted and don't even make it to the interview process. The selection process requires self-awareness and humility. Most carrier-based aviators have the "stick and throttle" skills to make the team. Humility and transparency are the characteristics of a good aviator.

After each flight, we went into the briefing room and debriefed the results of our training exercise: What was done well, what needed to improve, and how we would perfect our performance prior to the next flight. The video capturing each maneuver for debrief starts and ends with the hand salute. All six hands, up and down together.

Other Elements of a Team Force Multiplier

It's obvious that the proper use of technology and social media platforms such as LinkedIn, team websites, Constant Contact, HubSpot, and various customer relationship management (CRM) tools all help to leverage capacity and support sales and marketing efforts. You want to make it easy for potential clients to find you as well as tapping into the networks of your clients for referral opportunities. These capabilities cannot be ignored when considering the team's Force Multiplier Effect. Speed, efficiency, monitoring, and execution are all enabled if technology is used appropriately.

Another important key to collaboration is trust and transparency. Trust is a component of the Force Multiplier Effect. We have found that when team members trust one another and can rely on one another to execute the mission without hesitation, tasks are completed in a timely manner, which leads to goal accomplishment. Team members work in an environment characterized by open communication and information sharing. These are environments that thrive and retain team members. Team leadership must help team members to understand their capacity to collaborate both internally and externally. Individual creative ideas are necessary in team environments. Avoidance of "groupthink," meaning that the only promising ideas come from the team, can be an impediment to success and performance. Teams must be able to cross collaborate with other teams and individuals to nurture fresh thinking for team sustainability.

Team Challenge

Utilizing Figure 7.1, meet with your team and discuss potential collaborative relationships that might benefit your team. Assign a member of the team to explore these relationships and develop opportunities for collaboration. Measure your team's ability to collaborate both internally and externally. Discuss who on your team can create the Force Multiplier Effect.

NOTE

1. http://www.adaptabilitycoach.com/tag/force-multiplier-effect/.

CHAPTER 8

Shock Trauma Surgery Teams: A Compare and Contrast View

"I mean the reason I went into surgery is because I wanted to ride in on my white horse and save the day. I'm coming with my white horse and you better get out of my way because I'm going to save your life. Everybody who goes into this area does so because we want to save. So, when we lose it sucks. I hate that. If you're just as good as I am, you're not good enough. Your job is to be better than me."

—Andre Campbell, MD

Teams have different leadership styles and many ways to collaborate internally with other advisor teams, collaborating with a client's team of advisors, and collaborating with other specialty teams that may reside in other locations. We examined what could be learned from teams outside the realm of financial services. There are many teams that the financial services industry can emulate to improve leadership, collaboration, and performance. In fact, Wharton management professor Katherine Klein, PhD, conducted a 10-month study of surgery teams in Baltimore to fully understand surgical/trauma teams. The study was presented in a paper titled "A Leadership System for Emergency Action Teams: Rigid Hierarchy and Dynamic Flexibility," co-authored by Klein; Jonathan C. Ziegert, a visiting scholar at Wharton; Andrew P. Knight, a Wharton doctoral student; and Yan Xiao, a professor and lead researcher at the School of Medicine, University of Maryland, Baltimore. A compare and contrast view of trauma teams and financial advisor teams provides great learning examples.

There are several takeaways we are highlighting for financial advisor teams:

- The shifts in leadership among team members.
- The common vision that is characteristic of all trauma team members.
- Team organization in a crisis.

- Role identification and delegation of responsibilities among team members.
- The rotation of team members provides exponential learning.

We decided to do some of our own homework and interview Andre R. Campbell, MD. Dr. Campbell is affiliated with the University of California, San Francisco, School of Medicine, in the Department of Surgery. "My clinical practice is based at the Zuckerberg San Francisco General Hospital, also known as San Francisco General Hospital. Some people call it the General or some people just call it the County Hospital." He has been working there as an attending surgeon. He's been a senior surgeon, fully trained for now 23 years. He has a specialty in what is called trauma and acute care surgery, as well as general surgery. He is a board certified general surgeon and also board certified in surgical critical care. He performs general surgery, abdominal surgery, elective surgery, and trauma surgery. Dr. Campbell performs intensive care work, work in the intensive care unit (ICU), the emergency department, operating room – a lot of different venues – and he also has an elective surgery practice.

His official titles include professor of surgery at the University of California, San Francisco; medical director of the Surgical Intensive Care Unit at Zuckerberg San Francisco General Hospital; and attending trauma surgeon at Zuckerberg San Francisco General Hospital. He is a graduate of Harvard University, AB, and the University of San Francisco Medical School. His honors, awards, and credentials are too extensive to mention.[1]

Think about the following scenario that can happen on any given day. Imagine it's 2:30 in the morning. You are a trauma surgeon, and the accident victim has just been brought into the hospital with multiple gunshot wounds. The trauma team is ready to go. The airways are checked, breathing is checked, and the circulatory system is checked. This is real, and it's time to save a life.

This is life in the emergency department at the University of California San Francisco General Hospital and many trauma centers around the country. We wanted to understand both the leadership characteristics and the process by which trauma teams function. Our findings determined that there is a strong correlation among the activities of a trauma team, financial advisor teams, and teams in general. We believe through this comparison that there are lessons to be learned.

For example, as described by a trauma team member, "The initial treatment of patients is guided by routines or protocols that organize and prescribe the team's activities, protocols that the personnel observe and teach to others." One attending anesthesiologist described the Advanced Trauma Life Support manual as "the handbook we are singing from during the first 10 minutes of any resuscitation." Another fellow, referring to the manual's "ABC's of patient care," said: "To an outsider looking in, it looks like chaos. But everything is done in an orderly fashion. So, when a patient comes in, airway's first (A), breathing's second (B), circulation's third (C).... It all looks unorganized, but it's organized."[2]

In the context of financial advisor teams, these activities and protocols would be documented in the team's business plan and strategy document. This would be the equivalent of the surgical team's handbook. The commonality that we draw from the trauma team for the benefit of advisor teams is to parallel a set of routines and protocols for clients. For example, every client would receive a certain level of contact each year. They might have four client reviews, with two of the four reviews conducted in person. There might be a one-hour response to problems with a 24-hour resolution. Success in trauma is a prescribed process and way of doing things that is characteristic across all patients. Advisors can replicate this example by creating a prescribed client experience that is implemented across the board.

Trauma system means that there's a prehospital care: So it's the paramedics; it's the emergency care that's administered in the emergency department; it's the operative care that gets done; it's the ICU care afterward; it's the postoperative care, and the care after people are injured; and so it is reasonably the beginning to the end of your injuries. It's this collaboration of the external team members that helps to create the Force Multiplier Effect. Team members don't have time to second-guess the roles that each member or that of the specialists play in the saving of a life.

For financial advisors, it's leveraging the expertise of both in-house specialists or a client's team of advisors.

According to Dr. Campbell, "Our team consists of several people. It is usually one of the trauma attending surgeons of the day, and we have trauma fellows who are posttraining surgeons. That means that they've done a general surgery residency training program, which goes about five or seven years; if it's seven years, you're academic, five if not. And then it has surgical residents, usually fourth- or fifth-year residents. Third-year residents will be interns. We also have nurse practitioners on our team, and there will be medical students, a pharmacist, and other people who help us run the team. So it is not one person, it is a network of folks who basically take care of patients."

According to Professor Klein, "Our findings reveal a complex system in which the active leadership role shifts among team leaders arrayed in a hierarchy of expertise and experience. Enabled by structured routines, established tradition and values, expert support staff, and individuals' awareness of the passage of time, the leadership system facilitates swift coordination, reliable performance, and development of the team's least experienced members."[3]

The trauma team, headed by the trauma surgeon, goes to the emergency department; and, basically, combining with the emergency department personnel, the trauma surgeons with a trauma team – like the anesthesiologist, the radiologist, technician, the nurses, everyone else – come prepared to best care for the injured patient when they enter the emergency department.

The key takeaway for advisor teams is to allow leadership to shift based on the functional expertise of each team member. If each team member clearly understands his or her role, a fluidity in solving the complex problems of the client are at the forefront.

What are the dynamic changes occurring in the workplace that impact teams and especially advisor teams?

Advisor teams must utilize the leverage and capabilities of the entire organization. In trauma, depending on the immediate needs of the patient, specialists or specialty teams are called in to perform very complex surgeries. We find that true collaboration among advisor specialty teams can also achieve the desired results in complex client scenarios, for example, in estates and trusts or other intricate areas. As in trauma teams, these specialists or specialty teams work in areas that require improvisation to function well under challenging circumstances.

Campbell states, "The decision after they come and get assessed, the tools that we use are based on techniques that have been around probably about 35, 40 years now, called Advanced Trauma Life Support, or ATLS. ATLS is the bible on which we care for people. Pretty much every day we take care of people the same way. Basically, they come in, they get their airway assessed, we see if they're breathing, we check their circulation, we see if they can move or not. We take their clothes off, expose them, see where all the injuries are, look at all their extremities, their legs and arms, their head and neck, everything else, their body. We start then what's called a secondary survey, where we start from head to toe, and looking at the head, neck, chest, abdomen, pelvis, extremities, doing an assessment, and pretty much that's how everybody who gets injured in the United States is cared for when they come to a trauma center."

The takeaway is for financial advisor teams to conduct a detailed profile of the client and build a financial plan complete with strategies and goals. This seems very basic that all clients should receive this level of service.

Evolution of the Contemporary Workplace

The contemporary workplace is evolving rapidly. Work organizations now rely increasingly on interdisciplinary action teams – "highly skilled specialist teams cooperating in brief performance events that require improvisation in unpredictable circumstances." Further, the tempo of work is changing, becoming not only faster but also more dynamic and unpredictable.

Organizational complexity is increasing as well, as contemporary work organizations experience tighter coupling of their units and functions, necessitating highly reliable team and organizational performance. Finally, the employee–employer relationship is weakening. Given increasing employee turnover, long-term employee relationships cannot be assumed. The trauma surgery teams present a microcosm of many of the dynamic challenges that contemporary organizations face.[4]

There are many tools available for advisors for collaboration, allowing multiple parties to communicate virtually no matter where they may be domiciled. Documents can be viewed and edited by multiple parties. With the tools of collaboration continuing to evolve due to workplace productivity increasing, these tools are becoming more mainstream and often at a pace that is faster than many advisors can grasp or implement. We live in an instant response world. Clients and employees have no patience for inadequate or delayed response times.

Dr. Campbell aroused our curiosity after our initial conversation and we wanted to ask some questions that would provide some clarity on the activities of a trauma surgery team. We then compared those activities to financial advisor teams. What follows is the interview.

> The financial advisor team members/leader decide who to bring in for certain needs/markets (i.e., philanthropic work, tax planning, etc.) and examine the diverse capabilities of the members.
>
> Stated Dr. Campbell, "There's the trauma team and then there's the group of folks who care for the injured patients, and then we decide who else we need to help us, whether we need orthopedic surgeons for bone injuries; neurosurgeons for head injuries; urological surgeons for injuries to kidneys, urethra, or bladder; or any other specialists, head-neck surgeons, or plastic surgeons if we have soft tissue problems that we must deal with." So once those different professionals are involved in patient care, the trauma surgeon coordinates a larger team to apply their functional expertise.

So, let's talk about pretrauma for a moment in terms of how you know these folks, their competency levels. You've got this person who needs all this surgery; do you guys do a walk-through? From a practice drill and a rehearsal, how does that come together, pretrauma?

"There are no practice drills to go on. The only thing we really practice is that once a year we have a big disaster drill, where basically the whole city is involved with a disaster thing, and that's a formal thing. We don't really go through drills because everybody knows what their role is, and they understand that when the trauma attending surgeon rolls into the room, we oversee what's going on. If they are not so injured, then the evening physicians can do some of the work, but if they're severely injured, then the trauma surgeon is in charge."

The financial advisor team/members get together at a scheduled time and place to review accomplishments, business plan, onboarding, and so on, to confirm who is in charge and who does what in case of a special client need.

How about postsurgery follow-up? Once you've done what you needed to do, what happens postsurgery, who does the follow-up, and how is that handled?

"So, it depends on how long they're in the hospital. Some patients might stay in the hospital a long time depending on their injuries, and during that time what will happen is after they come into the emergency department, we decide whether they go to the operating room, the intensive care unit, do they go to the regular floor, or where do they go depending on what their injuries are. And that is based on a triage decision by the trauma surgeons in charge. Once that's decided, then that dictates what will happen. If they go to ICU, there's another team of ICU doctors and neurosurgeons if they have a head injury or other people to help us, and we'll work together. We coordinate all that

> care to make sure everything is done and they
> stay with us as long as they need to. Then what
> happens is after they recover from their injuries
> and we figure out what they can do, they can go
> to either rehab – rehabilitation, where they figure
> out how to get their lives back together again – and
> some people go home, depending on what's wrong
> with them and on what support systems they have
> available to them."

The financial advisor team determines what additional care and advice is needed for the client, for example, accountants, lawyers, insurance specialists.

"It's not my job, man!" Does this phrase sound familiar? Or is it your job? Your job is whatever the situation demands! We are in an era where some jobs cannot be described by a specific title. Perhaps this view can reimagine the thought process around traditional roles and responsibilities. The person with the best experience or capability does the task.

In the financial services arena, the more situations or experiences that team leaders encounter, the greater the likelihood for a positive outcome. Collaboration and the sharing of experiences with other teams can contribute to this experiential learning.

Activities of Effective Team Leaders

In examining team leader effectiveness, there are similarities shared by both trauma teams and advisor teams. Here are five of the most important attributes:

1. Monitor the team's performance and environment to discern threats to the team's effectiveness.
2. Structure and direct team members' activities, enhancing team member coordination and cooperation.
3. Teach and train team members, developing their skills and knowledge.

4. Motivate and inspire team members, fostering team members' commitment to task accomplishment.
5. Establish norms and routines that enable a positive and safe affective climate within the team.[5]

Delegation of Duties and Responsibilities

Trauma teams are organized vertically; however, they perform in a horizontal manner that is broken down in terms of the attending surgeon, the fellow, and the admitting resident. While there is a hierarchy of responsibility, leadership can shift among the three key positions. The nurses also play a key role in the checks and balances of delivering patient care. Why does this team effort work so well? This structure creates redundancy and enhances the reliability of patient care. If financial advisor teams can "get it right" by managing duties and responsibilities along with shifts in leadership, it will enhance team effectiveness.

In trauma, team leaders teach team members by actively giving – a lesson that certainly can be forged by all teams. If routines and protocols, it's like recorded history and knowledge – no time for experimentation. People know exactly what to do. Can this happen in financial services to elevate the client experience? We think so.

Summary

A key point that resonated with us during our conversation with Dr. Campbell was his deep sense of altruism. It was an attitude he brings into surgery that permeates with everyone in the operating room. They are there to save a life. This is his mission and that of his team.

An important aspect of surgical training is to "see one, do one, teach one" – that is, to see a procedure, do one (or more), and then teach others to do the procedure.[6] This mentoring process is embedded in the training that all residents receive.

This process should apply to onboarding new advisors as well. It would reduce costly industry turnover.

The challenge with team leadership is often the knowledge and best practices are not institutionalized, and if they *are* institutionalized there is no room for change or flexibility as the norms or external competitive threats evolve.

When new leadership comes in, he or she may want to change many strategies or practices. Why not build on existing protocols and capture the institutional knowledge? Create a knowledge library with videos, articles, testimonials, and training sessions. Prepare employees for change, and warn them ahead of time that everything is subject to change, thus creating a true learning environment.

Team Challenge

Schedule a team meeting and discuss the acceptable level of service or service model that every client should receive from the team. This includes the level of client contacts and portfolio reviews; planning and plan implementation, as well as the team's rapid response to client problems.

NOTES

1. www.surgery.ucsf.edu/faculty/general-surgery/andre-campbell, -md.aspx.
2. http://knowledge.wharton.upenn.edu/article/teamwork-in-a -shock-trauma-unit-new-lessons-in-leadership/.
3. Katherine J. Klein, Jonathan C. Ziegert, Andrew P. Knight, and Yan Xiao, (October 6, 2004) "A Leadership System for Emergency Action Teams: Rigid Hierarchy and Dynamic Flexibility." http://d1c25a6gwz7q5e.cloudfront.net/papers/1282.pdf.
4. Klein et al., "A Leadership System for Emergency Action Teams: Rigid Hierarchy and Dynamic Flexibility."
5. Klein et al., "A Leadership System for Emergency Action Teams: Rigid Hierarchy and Dynamic Flexibility."
6. Klein et al., "A Leadership System for Emergency Action Teams: Rigid Hierarchy and Dynamic Flexibility."

Team Contract and Agreement

"Unless both sides win, no agreement can be permanent."

—Jimmy Carter

There are "gives and gets" in every contractual relationship, and they need to be articulated and memorialized in writing. We have witnessed many teams struggle and spend lots of time deciding on compensation splits and who gets what in the team relationship. They lose sight of the big picture and potential growth opportunities. We're not saying that compensation isn't important as one component to overall team dynamics. You probably understand by now that most of the team challenge assignments are designed to get team members communicating prior to deciding on how the production credits are split and bonuses to members are paid. In any compensation structure or split, it's important that team members not be demotivated by compensation. Everyone should be compensated fairly for results.

Team members should come together over several sessions to discuss the wants, needs, and desires of each team member. Put everything on the table first before deciding on the final arrangements. The first meeting is a brainstorming session, and at the end of the session a summary of what was discussed should be distributed to each team member. Perhaps each of the team members have had a long-standing relationship and have a mutual trust for one another. This trust should be maintained well into the future of the team's existence. Defining the parameters of the working relationship is a key to maintaining this trust and keeping conflict at a minimum.

A team agreement is still an important dynamic in the over-all relationship. If team members cannot agree on some basic elements of an agreement, the team may be doomed from the start. The communication from the very beginning, concessions made by the parties, and compromises that should be made provide the basis for the working relationship. After all, this is a business relationship and should be organized as such.

You should speak with your **compliance department** and determine what contract templates might be available at your firm. There might be a final review by your administrative staff, branch manager, and your compliance department.

Some of the key elements to think about in your discussion with your team member(s) might include:

- Compensation and splits.
- Delegation of duties and responsibilities.
- Provisions in the event of a team breakup.
- Provisions for onboarding a family member.
- Provisions for the retirement of a team member.
- Provision for the sharing of team expenses and budget overruns.
- Provision for the resolution of conflicts; who's the final arbitrator?
- How will team decisions be made?
- What does it take for a team member to reach parity in compensation in the event of uneven splits?

Now let's talk about each of these key elements and how to make your team even stronger.

Compensation and Team Splits

Each team member should bring verifiable documents that indicate each team member's business performance. This will determine the baseline for determining current revenue splits and future revenue splits. Not all revenue or production is

Team member	Annualized production	Payout	Compensation	Equity split
Mary	$600,000	40%	$240,000	43%
Joe	$600,000	40%	$240,000	43%
Larry	$200,000	35%	$69,600	14%
Totals	$1,400,000		$$549,600	100%

Figure 9.1 Team compensation and revenue splits.

equal. There are variables to consider such as product diversification, and recurring revenue streams versus transactional business. Let's review the example in Figure 9.1.

In Figure 9.1, Mary and Joe have an equal production split. Larry is a new member of the team and is a junior partner. Mary and Joe can agree to help supplement Larry's production or compensation based on a performance criterion to further create an incentive for Larry to perform. Therefore, the equity split could be adjusted upward with a short-term decline in Mary and Joe's compensation. If they believe that Larry's value-add will be worthwhile for the team, they will be more open to making an investment in Larry by doing a forecast that substantiates the team's growth potential.

An important part of compensation and team splits is that you must first start with the verifiable documents that demonstrate each team member's performance. It will determine the baseline for how revenue splits and future revenue splits should take place, and it's also important to understand that not all revenue or production is equal. Someone may have a recurring fee revenue stream or more fee-based business that predominates the transactional business.

In other words, there is no guarantee that the person doing the transactional business would be able to repeat the amount of transactional business that could occur in the future. The variables to consider are product diversification and recurring revenue streams versus transactional business.

Delegation of Duties and Responsibilities and the Decision-making Process

We have previously discussed the need for teams to organize themselves by determining who is responsible for specific activities on the team. While you want to maintain flexibility in this regard, having a general sense of where responsibilities and decision making lie can help to avoid conflict in the future. Some of this information can be taken from the team's business strategy plan document.

A key area to consider is how the team will invest a percentage of its revenues back into the business. The team can consider items such as supplemental compensation for additional administrative support, sales and marketing expenses for client acquisition, special events, and seminars. We will discuss this in more detail in the Provision for the Sharing of Team Expenses and Budget Overruns section.

Provisions in the Event of a Team Breakup

For distinct reasons, a team may decide that they want to end the team relationship, so a contract needs to define what happens if the team members (or one team member) decide to go their separate ways. How will assets, households, and the budgetary issues be handled if this team decides to disband or get a "divorce"? Is it going to be based on the percentage ownership or revenue responsibility for each team member? Is it going to be based on who's the relationship manager for a certain household? Is it going to be based on shared revenue for a period of time? In any event, the team must sit down and discuss the breakup and make the determination, if there is a breakup and a conflict emerges, of how that conflict will be resolved. This is one of the elements of the team agreement.

Provisions for Onboarding a Family Member

Whether you are onboarding a family member or onboarding another team member, teams need to agree that the person being considered is the right person for the team. Assimilating another team member into your culture takes work. After all, the team has its ways, methods, and rituals of behavior that are second nature to existing team members. A new member should be oriented regarding the team dynamics over a period of time. They must agree on what the roles and responsibilities will be for this new team member with the allocation of team resources, assets, and revenue as well as how compensation is going to be allocated for a new member and how the team will agree on what the resource allocation is going to be for that new family member. Of course, you can't allow for everything that might come up, but you should have some of the basic items or provisions identified in the contract beforehand, and that reduces conflict as well.

Sometimes onboarding a family member flies in the face of another team member's effort to predetermine the ownership of team resources, households, and future revenue streams. Therefore, teams must meet and decide how those issues should be handled. Additionally, it's important to handle it early if a team is thinking this junior family member may potentially be seen as an equal owner of a team's resources, households, and assets. What we want to do is minimize that conflict. It could be a big problem and tug at the emotions of team members and lead to one team member's feeling that they've lost the shared ownership and want to dissolve the team.

Onboarding or recruiting additional team members raises the issue about what is the arrangement to determine how an additional team member is hired or brought onto the team, who provides input for selection, and exactly what the deciding factors are to determine whether somebody gets onboarded and hired by a team. All team members should participate in the interview and selection process. This involvement is important for team cohesiveness. It creates an environment where each team member feels that his or her input is valued.

Provisions for the Retirement of a Team Member

As an example, you have three team members, and one is more senior and decides he's going to retire or leave the business.

Is there a provision for a buyout of that team member and how it should take place and over what time frame? Some firms already have provisions for the retirement of a team member, so make sure you understand the policies of your organization with respect to retirements and buyouts of another advisor's practice.

But does the team member receive a certain payment for a specified period? Does the team member reduce his work hours and is he retained as an employee at a reduced workload to ensure the smooth transitions of those account relationships where he acts as the relationship manager to ensure that transition? That should be discussed up front. Each team member is a stakeholder in the business and, therefore, wants to realize some benefit for helping to build and grow the business and should be rewarded for his or her effort.

Provision for the Sharing of Team Expenses and Budget Overruns

Let's say you have one team member doing 60% of the revenue and another doing 40%. When it comes time for sharing team expenses, are you going to share them in a 60-40 split, or are you going to share team expenses equally? What are the guidelines that the team will start with for the sharing of the expenses?

If you have three team members and the revenue streams aren't equal but they all benefit from what the expenses create, is that the process? Sometimes these expenses might be in sales and marketing; it could be seminars or client appreciation events. Once the team determines the budget for the year, you are basically going to agree on the budget and how these expenses are going to be shared. Now, sometimes there could be an additional opportunity that a team can fund, so how is the decision going to be made for funding expenses that exceed the team's budget? If you agree up front, then you have a process and a procedure for determining budget or cost overruns. Obviously, there is always the potential for unforeseen circumstances or opportunities that may need to be funded by the team. If the team has a process for how these things will be handled, it can minimize potential conflict in the future.

Provision for the Resolution of Conflicts: Who's the Final Arbitrator?

Teams may have a conflict that comes up during the scope of their business activities. It could be who's going to be the key relationship manager on an account/household that the team has recently acquired? Or who should be responsible for going to a training program? It could be any number of issues that come up with the team. It could be issues such as work hours, availability for client meetings, and work schedule. Perhaps the team sits down and is unable to reach an agreement on how to resolve potential conflicts. Rather than break up, rather than agree to disagree, sometimes you just need someone to just step in as an outside third party to help resolve the conflict or provide a second opinion.

It could be the branch manager. It could be an outside person who's going to act as the final arbitrator for the conflict, or it could be the administrative manager in the office or the associate manager. This should be someone who can take an objective look at the issues and then help arbitrate or mediate the conflict with the team.

What you're doing in advance is agreeing that if a conflict/dispute should arise that can't be resolved by the team, then you have a process in place for the resolution of the conflict. The resolution of the dispute may be binding to the team based on identifying an administrator or manager within that office who will act as the final mediator or arbitrator and that the team agrees they will make the most appropriate decision.

How Will Team Decisions Be Made?

In our experience, a team should create a business plan and strategy document right away. Going through this initial process of communicating, making decisions, and determining if values and purposes are aligned provides excellent feedback as to whether individual team members can work together. Part of the rationale for this is that team members begin the process of sharing and agreeing on a lot of strategic decisions that the team is going to collectively abide by.

You're going to have these preliminary decisions and agreements, which are about the team members communicating with each other. Team members agree that they're going to work together and discuss these issues, and they will memorialize them in writing for more complex decisions that may come up in the future. The team has ritualized a go-to process on decisions that they've made and agreed to should memories become short as to what was agreed to by team members. This also reduces conflict and disputes.

In Chapter 5, "Establishing a Vision, Mission Statement, Value Proposition, and Elevator Pitch," we discussed the need for the team to have a clarified vision, value proposition, and mission statement. This is important to ensure that each team member is strategically aligned with its purpose. When conflict does emerge, the team can discuss whether the issue causing the conflict is consistent or inconsistent with the team's values and purpose.

What Does It Take for a Team Member to Reach Parity in Managing Uneven Revenue Splits

It's been our experience that sometimes the levels of production or revenue generated by team members might not be apportioned equally. Therefore, team members want to know how they reach a point where compensation is at parity or equal. When there is a producer or an advisor who is generating the lion's share of the production, gaining parity could take a long time – even years – for team members to reach their levels. Compare it to law firms where it can take years to make partner. One of the things you must look at: Maybe the senior producer on the team is slowing down or growing at 5% or 10% per year, and the younger team members are growing at 20% a year or more. They are going to want to know when and how they become equal partners in terms of the sharing of revenue or, at the very least, how compensation splits will be adjusted to reflect productivity growth.

An example could be if the team is doing $1.5 million in revenue and one team member is doing $1 million in revenue, perhaps the split doesn't occur until the entire team is doing $2.5 million in revenue. Then we reach the point where the revenue share is equal, and nobody is diminished by one team member receiving more in the way of production than the other.

You should begin to discuss early on among team members about the issue of parity, when it takes place, and under what circumstances it will happen.

Team Challenge

If you haven't reviewed your team agreement, make sure it has the most essential elements discussed in this chapter. Determine if your team agreement needs a review or an update.

10

The Key Drivers of Your Business, Forecasting Growth, and Building Your Business Plan

"Always have a plan, and believe in it. Nothing happens by accident."

—Chuck Knox

Here is an outline of the important key drivers of your business. We will discuss each one in detail following the list:

I. Assets generate recurring fee revenues
   A. Transactional model versus fee-based model
II. Return on assets (ROA) or velocity rate on those assets
   A. Total revenue divided by assets under management = ROA or velocity rate
   B. See Table 10.2
III. Number of households and household management
   A. Number of households that can effectively be serviced per team member
   B. See Table 10.3
IV. Planning and doing the deep dive
   A. Doing more because you have more time to uncover opportunities or problems and develop solutions
V. Stair steps to the stars (continuous upgrading of clients you work with)
   A. You can't work with everyone; decide what channel the client belongs in
   B. See Table 10.2
VI. Time and hours, billable hours
   A. 600,000 producer / 2,000 hours = 300 per hour
   B. 40% PAYOUT = \$240,000 in actual compensation / 2,000 hours = \$120 per hour
   C. See Table 10.4

A team will need assets that generate recurring fee revenues and, obviously, to create a predictable revenue stream. A transactional model doesn't allow a team to create predictable revenue streams. Based on market conditions and economic conditions, it is difficult to determine what the level of transactions might be for a client as a predictor of future revenues. So most teams are moving more toward a fee-based model while there's still some transactional business being done. Assets that generate recurring fee revenue streams are the fuel that creates the engine of growth for most advisor teams.

The teams must determine what is the actual return – what they receive in terms of ROA or what we call "velocity rate" on those assets. For some teams that can range anywhere from 50 to 100 basis points based on assets under management. The way we calculate that is by taking the total revenue the team brings in and divide it by the amount of assets under management, and that equals the ROA or the velocity rate (as we define it).

How do teams take some of the guesswork out of forecasting revenue growth? One way is for teams to think about the key drivers of business performance and the team's potential for growth over the next five years. The model for business performance is either acquiring more assets under management that will provide fee income or through household penetration or obtaining more revenue per household. See Table 10.1.

Table 10.2 illustrates the assets needed for the team to achieve specific levels of production based on a velocity rate

Table 10.1 Production growth rate – all team members

Annual Growth Rate[a]	Year 1 25%	Year 2 25%	Year 3 25%	Year 4 25%	Year 5 25%
Incremental team growth in production[b]	350,000	437,500	546,875	683,594	854,492
Total team production[c]	1,750,000	2,187,500	2,734,375	3,147,969	4,272,461

[a]In this case, the team is forecasting a 25% growth rate in team production.
[b]The incremental growth rate or increase in production is forecasted to be $854,492 by year 5.
[c]Total team production is forecasted to be $4,272,461 by year 5.

Table 10.2 Average velocity rate on assets

Rate	Year 1 0.80%	Year 2 0.80%	Year 3 0.80%	Year 4 0.80%	Year 5 0.80%
Assets needed (millions)	218,750,000	273,437,500	341,796,875	427,246,094	534,057,617

of 0.80%. In year 5, for example, the team needs $534,057,617 in assets to achieve $4,272,461 in production.

Once you determine what that velocity rate is, the team needs to know the number of assets to reach the team's desired revenue goals. You need to think about the number of households and how you manage those households to achieve results. If there are too many households and you can't quite deliver on the service model, you will reach diminishing returns. In other words, you have so many households that you can't provide the service needed, and you might start to see some defection of clients to another advisor.

Look at the number of households that can effectively be serviced by each team member. We estimate that the real number should be no more than about 100 per team member. More comfortably that number might be around 75 to 85 households that you can accommodate to provide an exceptional service. See Table 10.3.

This table illustrates the importance of managing household asset and revenue thresholds to impact growth in the future. This team has determined that the number of household relationships it can effectively or comfortably service is 85 households (HHs) per team member. This team member is using a service model of contacting clients 12 times per year (once per month), four reviews, with two of the four reviews being done in person. As new HHs are established, the team reassigns their least profitable households to another financial advisor or most appropriate business channel for servicing. At the end of five years, the team is still servicing the same number of HHs; however, assets per HH have increased from $6,863 in year 1 to $16,755 by year 5. (See the Supernova

Table 10.3 Maximum number of team-based accounts

John	Year 1 85	Year 2 85	Year 3 85	Year 4 85	Year 5 85
Mary	85	85	85	85	85
Kevin	85	85	85	85	85
Total NBR accounts	255	255	255	255	255
Average assets per account	$857,843	$1,072,304	$1,340,380	$1,675,475	$2,094,344
Average revenue per account	$6,863	$8,578	$10,723	$13,404	$16,755
Minimum acceptable revenue threshold for 25% GROWTH	$8,578	$10,723	$13,404	$16,755	$20,943

NBR = number.

website for a forecasting application that allows you to do a forecast and "what if" scenarios in a matter of seconds; www .Supernovaconsulting.com.)

The next thing that we look at when managing our households and bringing in new assets is to understand what the causal relationship is that allows you to do the deep dive. We believe that every client should have some sort of financial plan where the financial advisor is taking a holistic view of that client's needs and problem areas, and is beginning to identify solutions that make sense. The solutions go beyond pure asset management or investment strategy; they take into consideration the client's goals. Do they want education for their children, do they want to purchase a vacation home, do they want to work on a tax minimization strategy, or do they want to focus on estate planning, for example? It's doing the deep dive that allows the advisor to have the time to uncover opportunities and problems, and develop solutions for the client. That's what teams are focusing on as opposed to simply doing nonrepeatable transaction business with clients. As with most transactions, there is a low-cost provider willing to accommodate a transaction.

Stair Steps to the Stars

Another key driver is called "Stair Steps to the Stars." This is a method to help you segment clients to advisors who have a lower minimum level of assets they will accept than you. For example, if your minimum is $1 million and you have $250,000 clients, it might be time to hand those over to someone whose minimum is $250,000. Over time you continue to raise your minimum as you get more affluent clients and give up those smaller clients so you can give every client the same elevated level of service. You can apply the 80/20 rule to your book and examine your relationships that derive 80% of your revenue and begin to set a benchmark for the level of client that you want to try to grow and develop over time and bring similar clients under your management. For example, you look at the top 20% and you discover that the average productivity or average assets per relationship is your top 20, which is $2 million. You want additional clients of this nature that meet your acceptable threshold to really grow. However, you might set your benchmark, let's say, at $2.4 million or $2.5 million, so going forward you're adding incremental households that will do more business for you and grow the revenue stream of your practice.

Remember, the service that you give to the client who doesn't meet your minimum acceptable standard might take time away from the client who needs the service. If you agree on the service model you're going to provide, then the team must concede that they can't work with everyone. This is easy to say but difficult to establish benchmarks and targets that are acceptable. The team can decide there are a certain number of relationships they're willing to keep, and the advisors may want to keep them for many varied reasons. They might be a family member or relative of another substantial client. They could be children of a wealthy client, and you want to make sure that you have a relationship with those folks that might ultimately inherit the client's assets. That is part of the multigenerational planning that teams must incorporate in their practice.

The service challenges associated with a growing practice and providing the best client experience can be overwhelming.

As you clearly define the most suitable clients for your practice, you must continuously determine how many relationships you can effectively manage. If you accept too many relationships, providing an exceptional client experience is diminished. Therefore, a decision must be made to shift client management responsibilities to another advisor team that has the capacity to work with a specific level of client relationships or an alternative service model such as the firm's digital advice channel, if available.

The impediment to growing the practice is constant evaluation and reevaluation of what the team can handle in terms of households and in assets. A crucial decision that must be considered is whether the key methodology is either more assets or more households, but you must constantly be aware of how many households can be effectively managed.

In these situations, you might ask, "Who is managing the business?" Is the business running the advisor, or is the advisor leading and managing the business?

What Is Your Time and Billable Hours?

You want to look at your total revenue. If you have a $600,000 producer and on an annual basis they're able to work 2,000 hours per year, and you divided the number of hours by the amount of revenue, they're looking at $300 per hour. Now, if they looked at it in terms of their actual compensation, they might say, "Well, my payout on the $600,000 really results in $240,000 in actual compensation, divided by the 2,000 hours and the billable hours is really $120 per hour." See Table 10.4.

This case illustrates a three-person team with annualized production of $1,400,000. Total team compensation is $560,000. John and Mary are at parity, each having an equal share of the production. Kevin is a junior member of the team with a share of the production of 14%.

So now, the team member needs to collectively decide: What is my time worth? How do I spend my time? Who needs my services and how do I want to be compensated for a premium level of service? The value you provide should coincide with the compensation you receive or that your team receives.

Table 10.4 Team compensation and billable hours

Team member	Annualized revenue	Payout	Compen- sation	Equity split	Billable hours[a] / compen- sation	Billable hours[b] Revenues
John	$600,000	40%	$240,000	43%	$120	$300
Mary	$600,000	40%	$240,000	43%	$120	$300
Kevin	$200,000	40%	$80,000	14%	$40	$100
Total	$1,400,000		$560,000	100%	$93.33	$233

[a]Billable hours based on 2000 hours worked per year based on advisor compensation.
[b]Billable hours based on 2000 hours worked per year based on advisor revenues.

Teams must review the key drivers of their business. They must look at the assets that they're interested in bringing in and the number of households that they can effectively manage. They also need to look at the planning that they can do for those households and make some decisions about who they can work with in terms of the time that they spend on each relationship. What is their value-add in specific relationships? There are times in which a team must work with a smaller relationship such as a relative of an affluent household or a center of influence that refers significant relationships to the team. In cases like this, a team must make an accommodation because it makes good business sense to do so.

The team challenge, then, is for the team to sit down, do an assessment of current team performance, gain an understanding of the key variables that impact revenue and performance, then discuss performance goals with each team member and decide how many households they can effectively manage or service.

It's been said that "what gets measured gets accomplished." The whole idea here is that if you don't measure against certain specific performance criteria or metrics, how do you know if you've arrived at your destination? Oftentimes, we find that people don't want to be held accountable for performance in metrics because they don't want to set themselves up for failure – all the more reason why teams must have a specific team strategy to help them get to where they want to go.

It's said that there's no shame in failure because he or she who has never failed is one who has never tried. The idea is to get the team to discuss the key variables that impact revenue and performance.

Outline for a Team Business Plan and Strategy Meeting

All teams should have a business plan that serves as a point of reference or guidepost for how the team intends to operate. If you currently do not have a plan, the following outline will provide most of the elements to include in your business plan and strategy document. Adjust the plan to the focus of your team.

    I. Vision

  II. Mission statement   One page

 III. Elevator pitch

 IV. Value proposition   Key is to get everyone aligned
       with steps 1–4

  V. Strategy

    A. Strengths

    B. Weaknesses – gap analysis   One page

    C. Opportunities

    D. Threats

 VI. Five Star Model – delegation of duties and responsibilities

    A. Planning

    B. Implementation   One page

    C. Brand

    D. Marketing

    E. Leadership/Accountability

VII. Goals/Activity goals   One page

    A. Client acquisition

       1. Prospects

       2. Centers of influence (COIs)

       3. Mastermind groups

       4. Enthusiastically Endorsed Model

       5. Nonprofit community boards

       6. Key performance indicators (KPIs)[1]

      B. Service/Retention
         1. 12-4-2
         2. Agendas/Client service agendas
         3. Penetration
         4. Net new money
         5. Planning
         6. Products and investment services   12- to 24-month agenda
         7. Sales forecast utilizing the forecast tool
VIII. Action plan   Two to three pages
      A. Initiatives – no more than five
      B. Tasks
      C. Timing
      D. Responsibilities
      E. Sales forecast tool review   30 minutes to 1 hour
  IX. Team effectiveness checklist   Review
   X. Executive summary

Please provide a succinct overview of your plan, one paragraph max.

Team Challenge

Do an assessment of current team performance. Understand the key variables that impact revenue and performance. Then discuss performance goals as a team. (We have a tool that can help you do this within minutes.) Draft your team's business plan and strategy document.

NOTE

1. www.kitces.com/blog/what-are-the-key-performance-indicators-kpis-for-your-financial-planning-firm/.

11

Recruiting, Hiring, and Retaining Good People

"Take my assets, leave my people, and in five years I will have it all back."

—Alfred P. Sloan, Former Chairman
and CEO of General Motors

I (Rob) cannot stress enough how important the hiring process is to your business and for building a successful team. Finding immense talent isn't as simple as people think. All industries are competing for talent. Rarely does high-quality talent come looking for you. Here, leadership is essential, and people who are effective team leaders have less turnover than poor leaders.

So how does a great leader hire?

A Commitment to Excellence Versus Accepting Mediocrity

The best way to begin this process – no matter how difficult it has been in the past – is to start fresh. Do not repeat the mistakes of the past. And one of the most common mistakes people make is to accept the best of what they've been offered rather than hiring the best person for the job. It's essential to take the time to find the *very best* candidates for the position rather than just accepting the candidates who might be available. If you don't do this, you will appear to your team as a person who doesn't care about them. Hiring "A-team players" raises the bar of performance for everyone.

I learned this lesson from one of my associates. I had consistently preached our core value of commitment to excellence and was in the process of hiring a new administration manager for the district when I realized this truth. The firm had sent me four candidates, and after exhaustive interviews by our entire team, I was about to hire the best of the four. My service manager, Kelly Anderson, came to me and said, "Rob, you're accepting mediocrity. You're accepting the best of what's been offered. You're not hiring *the best*. We both know Bob Smith is the best person for this job, and we should be hiring him."

Much to my dismay, she was right. After taking a moment to recover, I told her that I'd never been so proud of her. It took a lot of courage for her to confront me and protect our team from making a critical mistake. Everyone agreed that Bob was much better – he was from the area, he understood me, he knew our team and had had the guts to stand up and put his career on the line for us with national sales numerous times. Bob had just taken the job of being an admin manager in the Michigan District in the past six months, and I had already been turned down once by national sales in recruiting him. They had said, "No way, he just went in there." I picked up the phone, called the national admin manager, and said, "Don, we're accepting mediocrity; we want Bob Smith and I don't care what it takes to get him." We ended up getting Bob and, to this day, I don't know how we did it. With his help, we continued to be a top district in the country, and Bob was my greatest advocate – and is still doing an excellent job for the Midwest market.

This story of "commitment to excellence" became a part of the folklore of our culture.

Living your values is much harder than just preaching them. But when you live your values, you will be proud of every decision you make.

A commitment to excellence is essential, and taking the time to find excellence is vital to that commitment.

Here's my strategy for great hiring.

Sourcing the Candidate

Become great at identifying talent! Before you do anything, first decide what it is that you really need. If you had a magic wand, what are the exact qualities of the person that you need? Once you know what you want and need, how do you find that perfect candidate for your team?

- Begin with referrals from teammates. For both my client associate (CA) and financial advisor (FA) positions, 90% of my hiring came from introductions and referrals. They knew what I wanted and what we needed for the operation. That filter takes care of a huge amount of potentially wasted time.
- The next best source is referrals from people in your company: Your office staff, your region, and national sales. Getting the word out can uncover a highly qualified candidate interested in transferring.
- Referrals from clients can be excellent. A lot of clients have kids that would be a good fit. There are a lot of opportunities there, and they wouldn't refer you unless the person was suited to the job. They know you're a top-notch team and want you to have the best people; it's in their self-interest as well.
- Family members (see Onboarding).
- LinkedIn is your network and a suitable place to post the opening. Ideally, you know all your connections and can easily call with any questions.
- Referrals from your local university's business school can be a great resource for an intern. Talented interns can turn into talented teammates. We recommend always having at least one intern on staff. Think long term and strategically, not just tactically.

Identify Your Best Candidates

Then, of course, you'll want to screen the applications for *exactly* what you want. Ideally, you'll be able to identify five of the best candidates from this group, and then it's time to interview.

Take Time to *Really* Interview

Six steps for successful interviewing are:

1. Take the necessary time. Give yourself an hour for each interview.
2. Have at least three people interview the candidates to provide diverse points of view.
3. Keep your mind open, and don't decide in the first few minutes of the interview. Many interviewers make up their minds in the first three minutes of an interview and spend the rest of that interview confirming their initial decision. If you do that, you're not really interviewing. Human beings have an enormous need to be "right," even when they're wrong. It is one of the most common – and destructive – impulses in our society. When you go with that instinct, you're just confirming your initial opinion and giving in to that need to be "right." You may be excluding potentially good candidates and including potentially inferior candidates who made a great first impression. Give each person a chance to prove their worth.
4. Listen to learn, not to respond. Most interviewers talk way too much during interviews. Have a script of pre-planned questions. Ask the questions, listen, and probe. "What else?" "Why?"
5. How should the interview progress? Ninety-five percent of the interview time should be about the candidate. You're there to listen and to ask questions. Start with questions about a business experience (Tell me about your jobs: How did you transition and why? What did you learn from each of those jobs that made you the person you are today? What did you do well and not as well – failures as much as successes?), then move on to educational experience (What were you like in high school? Who did you hang out with? What were your strengths?). Move on to college (Where did you go? Did you play sports? Transfer? Fraternity or not?

What were you good at and not?). Next, overall strength and weakness (What things energize you? Tell me some stories about overcoming challenges.). I want to pick up any conflicts that I may have missed during school and work discussions. Then, hobbies and free time?

6. Ask questions: Do you have any questions that can I answer? Have they done their homework? Have they googled the company, read the annual report? Do they know about the job? Do they really want the job?

Then ask yourself: Can I relate to this person? How has this person handled conflict and stress? You really want to get to know the person beyond the resume and application.

Hold on to this information. The three interviewers should then compare notes and decide which candidates are a good fit for our team/company. Move forward with the top **three** people.

Check References

If you're going to hire someone, call the people who work for them and find out what are they like to work for. You'll want to speak to an employer and ask what she or he was like, but the people who will really tell you the truth are their peers. I always had my admin managers call their admin managers and my service managers call their service managers. I learned this lesson the hard way. I had a strong candidate on paper. The interview went well, and I called his boss, who gave him a glowing recommendation. Unfortunately, his boss lied to me to get rid of him. He turned out to be not right for our team. But that mistake led to a great lesson for us: Always check with the peers and direct reports!

Time for Dinner

The last step: Dinner. It may seem too intimate, but when I was hiring an FA or manager, I would have my final candidates over for dinner with their spouses. This takes time, but it can bring you closer to the perfect hire and protect you from disaster. For example, I was recruiting an FA from the competition and invited him and his spouse over for dinner at our home. I really liked him and thought he would be a good fit, but during dinner, he was so mean and rude to his wife that I didn't even consider hiring him.

Onboarding

Onboarding is vital to the success of your training program. My colleagues have heard me say this for years: You should treat every person you hire as if it's your best friend's son or daughter. And I looked at every firing as a personal failure, so you want this process to be seamless at every level. As with interviewing, take the time to properly onboard your new hires.

Set clear expectations. It's important to explain exactly what it is you want them to accomplish and exactly what you and they would like to get out of the job. Take time with them. Make them feel comfortable. Take them around the office and introduce them to every person.

Have someone take them out to lunch. Generally, make them feel welcome.

Begin the contents of their Supernova folder, including the personal and professional goals that they want to accomplish in the next 12 months.

Hiring family members is such an emotional topic, and perhaps this issue needs its own chapter due to the many complexities involved. The worst thing you can do for a newborn chick is to help it out of its shell. The same is true for children of FAs. Be at least as diligent in your hiring regimen with them as you would be on any new hire. I recommend being tougher because they and their peers will always think they had it easy because of Dad or Mom. Let them earn what they get, just like any other FA. Keeping a failed son or daughter FA around is humiliating and not fair to them. Making your candidate's son or daughter follow the process outlined below will at least give them a good start so they feel they have earned their position.

Begin Coaching Immediately

The first three to six months – when new hires are particularly susceptible to turnover – are most critical. On average, companies lose 17% of their new hires during the first three months.[1]

Coaching is vital at the very beginning of the onboarding process. Start by helping the new team member immediately build their business plan. Giving people the attention and direction they need is essential. It is your responsibility to enable your team to reflect positive core values. *The Supernova Advisor* can help immensely in this task by focusing on frequent communication, clear expectations, and accountability – this is the Supernova Process.

I suggest checking in with your new hires every day for the first 20 days to make sure everything is going as planned. FAs must develop their service model, marketing plan, financial planning model, and investment model, and study for the Series 7. It's a lot to get done in very little time. Once they finish the Series 7, I would meet with them weekly with a written agenda created by them for the first six months. After six months, I would meet monthly using the 12-4-2 Supernova Leaders Process.

There's a dramatic difference between having a coach and not having a coach. A typical trainee focuses on one thing and only one thing – passing the Series 7. If you don't pass it, you don't start. But typically, once they pass the exam, they must focus on developing a marketing plan and writing a business plan. The average talented FA can walk and chew gum at the same time. She can study for the Series 7 while building a business plan and developing niche markets, mastermind groups, and centers of influence, and can be huge leaps ahead of the other trainees. If you have a coach, it's much easier to do these things at once.

I recently worked with a new FA who hired me as a coach before he even had a job in the industry. Every week we made a list of priorities from the most important to the least important. We reshuffled the priorities depending on the pressing needs of the week. For example, he was concerned about the firm politics, office politics, location, and potential teaming. Each week we had a call and he created the agenda ahead of time, which would give me time to evaluate his priorities and consider different solutions. The office politics were the least important thing he had to focus on ... it sounds like a small thing, but it was a huge thing in terms of focus and concentration. I often helped him to realign his focus on real priorities and get rid of the distracting thinking (wasting of time on issues that he couldn't control or were irrelevant to him at this stage of the business). By coaching him weekly, I could help him to get back on track and focus on the things that he could control, like his self-assessment, and create his business plan and strategy. Well, he passed with flying colors and is on his way to becoming a great financial advisor.

So how do you coach your team members? Just as a refresher and for those who haven't yet read *The Supernova Advisor*,[2] the team leader builds a folder for each member of the team and meets with each of them monthly for 60 minutes to review their personal and professional development, their role and responsibilities, and their success and challenges in achieving those goals. Each team member has their folder with their personal and professional development plan, their role and responsibilities, and their business plan for how to achieve their respective goals and any challenges they've faced in accomplishing those goals.

With these monthly check-ins, you're going to avoid communications problems. And if it's not a good hire, you have 90 days to make a change, but you will have committed so much time and energy up front, you shouldn't have a problem.

When you're coaching your team, it's like five team members swimming down a pool at the same time, each having their own roles and responsibilities. No one is sitting on the side of the pool watching everyone else swim. Everyone is committed all day doing their respective job. Without this delegation and accountability, productivity is lost and morale suffers. There should be no difference, whether the leader is present or not.

Everyone should know his or her roles and responsibilities and be able to execute them brilliantly and independently.

A former Merrill Lynch manager, Larry Biederman, used to say, "You can't expect what you don't inspect." So giving your teammates your time and respect will result in consistently high morale. Again, you're creating a commitment to excellence on every level. Holding your team accountable will get high results. It takes time and courage, but it's worth it. If you treat each teammate with the same level of importance that you would for each client, you'll develop great relationships that are built on clear communication, expectations, and accountability.

Firing (Otherwise Counseling Out of the Role)

I can't say this enough: Hire well so you don't have to terminate people. And if you must terminate a team member, you need to take responsibility and examine how you can avoid doing it in the future.

Boston Massacre

After the 2008 recession, the Boston office manager of a major firm called 15 people in and terminated them all – 15 new people who had given up their previous lives to join this firm and thought it was the greatest opportunity in the world. If they had to terminate 15 people at once, they should have terminated the manager, too! If they were such poor hires, he was ultimately responsible. The costs and resources to the firm for bringing in 15 people was probably $3 million, not to mention the cost of human happiness. He potentially ruined all those lives. I thought it was one of the worst things I'd ever heard about in our industry. Were they all that bad? Then why were they hired? If they weren't and they just did it for economic reasons, it's just horrible. Years later, it still upsets me. If I had to terminate 15 people at once, I would have resigned. Hold yourself responsible and accountable for your positive hiring experiences and learn from those that don't quite work out.

Andy Edelman was a district director for Merrill Lynch for more than a decade. He was a Marine and demanded excellence in our business. Although he had a reputation for being tough, he was very good at hiring and training. His retention rate was twice the firm average, and his FAs were very loyal to him. How did he do it? He personally did the training when he was an office manager and made training a very critical objective when he ran the district. There might have been delegation, but there was never abdication under Andy. Andy always knew it was more than pride and culture; it was economic. Success in hiring means generations of revenues; failure means economic disaster.

Because of poor hiring results, most firms have gone through a process of hiring new candidates directly onto teams. Edward Jones had impressive results with their mentoring program, where a senior FA would reassign smaller accounts to a new hire. This dramatically improved the new candidate's success rate and freed up the senior FA to grow his or her business. This began as a beta test but quickly grew into an institutionalized program that paid for itself many times over.

When done thoughtfully with structure, this type of teaming can work well for everyone.

So you see how essential hiring, mentoring, and the teaming processes are to the success of your business.

What happens when you discover that you made a mistake hiring, a teammate has changed, or the team just isn't functioning properly due to irreconcilable differences?

If it's a partner who needs to be terminated or your team breaks up, you should take a long look at what your process was for forming your team and bringing on new advisors and additional partners. Unfortunately, most people hire or add someone to their team based on whether they like the person or trust the person, but that leaves out the full hiring process illustrated earlier. Divorces and team dissolutions are traumatic and can have a negative impact on trust in the relationship. As a manager, I knew that just because a team breaks up doesn't mean that those FAs wouldn't make great partners for someone else.

Typically, FAs that are willing to team once are excellent candidates for future teaming opportunities.

Let's look first at why teams break up before we put those FAs back on the horse. This is covered in great depth in Chapter 13, "Team Dysfunction: The Elephant in the Room." However, following are some points to consider.

Is This an Irreconcilable Difference?

Keeping a team on the solid ground, one only needs to review some of the marriage research by John Gottman, professor emeritus in psychology. One of his six predictors of divorce is a lack of respect. After decades of research videotaping 130 newly married couples in his "Love Lab," he found that if one or both people showed contempt while resolving their conflict, the probability was higher that their marriage would end in divorce.

It's all about **respect.**

When we look beyond the qualities of like and trust, what would cause us to lose respect for our teammate?

1. Work ethic or trust of calendar integrity: The work ethic is an understanding and agreement that your team members have with each other. Violating this and what I call trust of calendar integrity (being late for meetings or missing them) creates a lack of respect. In other words, not doing what you say you're going to do when you say you're going to do it. Trust starts with showing up for meetings, showing up for work, just showing up! Trust is built by doing what you say you are going to do when you say you will do it. Breaking that trust is a trust buster. Enough trust busters and clients leave, spouses leave, and teams break up.

I always ask people, "Do you think that you're a trustworthy person?" They respond, "Of course." "Do you ever break trusts?" They respond, "Never." Then I ask, "Have you been late in the past week? In the past day?" Being late demonstrates a lack of respect and a lack of importance in the relationship. When you are late, you didn't do what you said you were going to do, when you said you would do it. By doing that, you're saying that your time is more important than your client's/partner's time.

2. Lack of respect and even contempt: When lack of respect moves to contempt, the game is over.

I recently met with a team in Florida. They discussed with me the sad, abusive behavior from the senior partner. They said their team was like a family, but he doesn't tell us where he is. He isn't on time for meetings. He's started his own business and is spending all his time with the hope that it will pay off in the very near future. He is on time for meetings regarding that business but ignores his partners and takes them for granted. The senior partner is the rainmaker and the majority owner of the business. They care for him but don't see things changing. Unless there is a dramatic turnaround by the senior partner, this team is doomed to divorce. The other partners are like an abused spouse. They'll get to the point where they've had enough, then it is over.

3. Lack of communication and a lack of understanding/ listening: "My partner never talks to me and doesn't understand me." It's the same reason clients leave. You would hear statements like, "My FA doesn't call me" or "She doesn't understand who I am." This is particularly common on vertical teams where the senior partner does most of the business. Because the leader doesn't really lead, the team gets more and more frustrated by the lack of direction, vision, accountability, and recognition.

4. Acceptance of mediocrity/lack of respect for the team: One or more members of the team have checked out. In the Navy, we called it "ROAD – retired on active duty." You see it all the time. What happens when old Joe is a part of your team? You can ignore it or confront it. If you confront it, be sure you have a game plan for whatever reaction Joe has. Joe can do one of four things. Fight you, adopt a passive-aggressive compliance, change and make a renewed commitment to the team, or quit. I have seen all four reactions. If you value Joe and your team's commitment to excellence, you have no choice but to challenge Joe and hope Joe values you and the team more than his ego.

The Difficult Decision

If you've determined that you have an irreconcilable difference, what next?

You must eliminate this team dysfunction. In the case of the Florida team, the choice was for an individual member to leave the team or make a leadership change to keep the team from failing. Having difficult conversations about a team member's behavior or performance is never easy. However, a failure to have the conversation undermines the values, culture, and the performance of the entire team.

First, **ask for permission** to provide feedback and schedule time for this important purpose. Let the team member know that you must **provide feedback** that is difficult to share. The best feedback is straightforward and simple. Make the employee aware of the positive impact a change in behavior will have on the team. The team member must understand that no change in behavior is detrimental to the team. Next, reach an agreement as to the expected changes that need to occur. Finally, establish a scheduled time frame to review progress on the desired behavioral changes. You should be able to outline expectations and explain how your team member(s) are missing the mark. Performance reviews are a way to evaluate if certain goals or objectives are being met. Having fact-based evidence leaves less room for interpretation. I think it's important for team leaders to look inward and ask themselves a very fundamental question: Am I providing the right environment and opportunity for this individual to succeed? If not, you have some work to do before you terminate someone.

When putting someone on probation, what should they expect?

In the case of the Florida team, the second-in-command and the CSA (administrative assistant) need to discuss probation with the manager to get management support. Then they need a meeting to give a probation letter to the senior person that states clear expectations with accountability and a meeting every month. A 90-day probation doesn't have to last 90 days, by the way. If after 30 days, there is no change in behavior, you can terminate the person from the team.

Now That You're at the Point of Termination

The biggest error in terminating a team member is procrastination – in other words, prolonging the agony of having a difficult conversation and making difficult choices. We never have difficult conversations over a meal. If you engage people in this manner over a meal, they will have an expectation that lunch or dinner with you will not be pleasant. Once you have provided the coaching and the counseling and taken all the necessary steps to enable the team member to improve and all your efforts have been in vain, now you are prepared to make the difficult decision. Whenever possible, seek a partner in human resources to avoid potential legal liabilities. I like to say, "Help them find something that they are better suited to do." Treat people with dignity. They will speak highly of you and your firm in the community in which you reside.

Team member feedback should occur on a regular basis. It would be inappropriate for a team member to discover toward the end of a calendar year that he or she has been performing at a marginal level.

Team Challenge

Bring the team together and discuss the talent gap on the team. Create a checklist of attributes necessary for the new potential team member(s).

NOTES

1. https://www.shrm.org/resourcesandtools/hr-topics/talent-acquisi tion/pages/onboarding-key-retaining-engaging-talent.aspx.
2. Robert D. Knapp, *The Supernova Advisor: Crossing the Invisible Bridge to Exceptional Client Service and Consistent Growth* (Hoboken, NJ: John Wiley & Sons, 2008).

12

Onboarding and Mentoring a New Team Member

"If you cannot see where you are going, ask someone who has been there before."

—J. Loren Norris

Onboarding is the process of acquiring, accommodating, assimilating and accelerating new team members, **whether they come from outside or inside the organization.**[1]

We want to highlight how important onboarding and mentoring a new team member is for team growth, productivity improvement, and filling out team gaps. Let me share a story. A manager had recently recruited a competitive hire from another firm. This new hire previously had been a very successful producer, close to a million dollars, when he decided to go back and get a master of business administration (MBA) from an Ivy League school. On returning to his firm, he was awarded with an international assignment.

When the assignment was over, he didn't have another one, so he decided to go back into production at another, smaller firm. He knew under the "new reality," a team approach was the way to go. After working in that office for more than a year, there wasn't a suitable team arrangement forthcoming, so he was recruited and hired by another well-known firm. The branch manager at that firm positioned him to interview with a few teams, and there were a couple of teams that really showed an interest and wanted to work with him.

Both teams were interested in having him focus exclusively on bringing in new clients while they helped bring on these new relationships and assist with planning and money management. Neither team wanted to initially share clients or split production and assets. Instead, they recommended a split on new business, which favored existing team members and very little to the new advisor.

Some of the facts have been abbreviated; however, this is the basic story. What's wrong with this model? Clearly, the team really didn't know how to onboard a new team member, and the fact that the manager wasn't involved in the process creates some bigger issues and dysfunctions relevant to the team. We want to avoid landmines that can demotivate a new team member. Let's talk about how we can make some improvements to the process.

Onboarding a new team member is the equivalent of bringing an outsider into a new culture that has its own mores and folkways or rituals as identified in previous discussions. Here are some steps and thoughts to think about new team member onboarding. We will discuss them in-depth with solutions following the bulleted list:

- Don't start with production splits.
- Immediately start treating this person and communicating with them as a team member.
- Discuss your team strategy and where they see themselves contributing to the success of the team.
- Let each team member meet one-on-one with the new candidate.
- Let the new candidate ask questions about the team.
- Develop an integration strategy for the new team member.
- Do make quantitative assumptions about the value-added production lift that this new team member can provide.
- Decide on fair compensation during the onboarding process.
- Discuss the elements of an agreement.

When a team makes the decision to look for a new team member, the first thing they need to identify is the type of individuals that are needed, some of the responsibilities this new team member will help with, and how to integrate this team member into the overall business strategy. It's all about assimilating a new team member onto the team.

First, at least one member of the team should act as a mentor to this new team member and guide and welcome aboard this person to the new team. Instead, in this case, they immediately went to, "How do we revenue share?" as opposed to thinking about, "What is our basic business strategy? What's our plan? What are some of the areas that this dynamic person can really help us with?" Then begin to set forth a plan of action.

When you immediately begin talking about production splits and revenue sharing, you put in everybody's mind an expectation of a return right away. And this detracts from the real focus and the real strategy of what a team is attempting to do in terms of their direction.

The team must ask these questions:

- What is our integration process so we know where this new person might add some value?
- What are their capabilities and where they may add some incremental value to what we're already trying to accomplish?
- Does this person have some unique skills – like retirement expertise – that we don't have?
- Do they have relationships in the marketplace we could capitalize on if we had joint meetings?

There should be a very detailed interview process, and a lot of the work should be done up front with the team.

Oftentimes, teams will recruit a team member to build out the existing capabilities or further develop a niche market. This means, for example, a team may see the value of having someone with philanthropic and nonprofit expertise on their team or expertise in small business owners. Having this kind of experience and relationships will help bring on additional revenues within the niche.

The team needs to spell out the involvement of this team member and how they plan to integrate him or her into the team's structure. That may be an area of specialty for the new team member, but he or she may not have the intellect for or the capacity to support the team in that area. While the specialty is important, it may be required that the team member also understand asset allocation and some of the other service capabilities that can be developed for the team. Smaller teams need multidimensional team members, and they can create more specialized functions as business opportunities present themselves.

In the example at the beginning of this chapter, this didn't happen. The team members just saw a "body" and, roughly speaking, thought this was simply going to be another cobbled-together solution. The team really needed to first spend time on defining what their integration process was going to be. All the team members must be on board with that integration process, including the client associate. When this new team member comes on board and is requiring some additional work, the client associate understands exactly what needs to be done for that new team member. It could be simple things like becoming familiar with the technology, getting business cards, moving through the entire human resources new-hiring process. The engagement should involve four team members, and they should write this down in terms of the team integration process. "What is our engagement here with this new team member?" This is a question that must be answered.

The next thing the team must do is begin to set performance goals that focus on the key drivers that we've been talking about in our discussions: Goals for asset acquisition, client acquisition, and any skills we want this team member to pursue, such as a focus on the retirement plan segment of that team's current business, special planning capabilities, or insurance capabilities. Who on the team is going to take responsibility for the mentoring of that team member? Who is going to show that team member how things work on the team? Who will decide what the value proposition is, what our mission statement is, and what our elevator pitch is in terms of fully integrating and aligning this new team member to the overall strategy of the team?

The engagement should include going on appointments with this team member and an introduction of the team member to some of the team's existing household relationships. It should also involve the sharing of some household relationships via production or revenue splits. Once you start to share revenue, you become a stakeholder in this new team member's success. After that has been accomplished, we start to think about what would be a fair and equitable revenue-sharing arrangement for this new team member. In terms of delegation of duties and responsibilities, also provide a checklist for this new team member. Who does what on the team is vital.

Communication Is Critical: Don't Rush the Process

Many team members have a reluctance to sharing assets and revenues until new team members have proven themselves. That's understandable. It's challenging work getting some of the client relationships. Giving up part of their revenue stream seems counterproductive and counterintuitive, but the team needs to look at becoming a stakeholder in the success of this new team member. They need to understand that bringing on this new team member and sharing revenue is part of the process of making an investment in the new team member. Their reluctance is due to the uncertainty of whether this new member will succeed. You must assess your hiring risk and try to remove the barriers that stand in the way of this new team member's becoming successful. Then be prepared if there is turnover and the team member doesn't quite work out. There is no foolproof way to hire people, and perhaps a short probationary period might make some sense.

It's understandable, but the attitude on the part of all team members should be that they're making an investment in this person and desire for the new member to succeed. The attitude is this: "We will provide our resources and our capabilities to ensure the success of this new member. This team member is not going to be alone. This team member is going to be welcomed with wide open arms and be fully supported to ensure her success."

Now, it's important that the team helps this new team member get established very early. After all, if you put yourself in the shoes of the new member, you realize she wants to start contributing. She wants to feel that she is a part of the team.

She wants to feel welcome. If you skip a lot of the steps in the very beginning, it's going to impact the assimilation of this team member down the road. An effective way to think about this is to treat the new team member as an outsider who has just shown up midway into the school year, doesn't know anybody, and is trying to get familiar with how things work, where to go, where her locker is, and how to get some of these things done. You want to treat this new team member well and enable her to find her way. A team leader needs to reinforce that everyone wants to make this person feel inspired (i.e., we want to help her) and we want to enable accommodation of this new team member. We want to assimilate her into the team as quickly and as effectively as possible.

It's important to identify people inside the office environment that will be the "go-to" people for this new team member. This is how she can get questions answered. If you want to identify the outside resources that this new team member can take advantage of, that will also help with the onboarding process. The team should have a personal onboarding plan, with announcements such as, "Mary has just joined us as a new team member, and some of her responsibilities will be the following on our team." That way, if a team member is out of the office and Mary answers the phone, it's not like there is a stranger on the other end of the phone.

You don't want your new team member to be the odd person out. She needs to be comfortable with the strategies of the team, comfortable with the game plan, and involved in the practice so that the team receives the most value of bringing on a key member. These are the activities that are so important: Team meetings, the huddle sessions, and establishing developmental timelines of what's going to occur in the first week, the second week, the first 30 days, the first 60 days, the first 90 days, and the first 120 days while you onboard this new team member.

If you think about the military, when they onboard a new recruit, they teach him everything: How to look, how to dress, when to wake up, when to go to sleep, how to salute, all the rituals; all the values are expressed to that recruit in training. If you think of a basketball team, like the Golden State Warriors, who brought in key player Kevin Durant from Oklahoma, well, they're not bringing him in to sit on the bench. They want to integrate this guy into the whole team structure.

Let Your Candidate Ask Questions

I think it is crucial for you to let your candidate ask questions. In the example we have been discussing, the team really didn't share any of the dynamics about the team, their markets, their niches that they go after, their production, or their velocity rates. It's essential that the new candidate has an opportunity to also interview the team.

Find out about team member backgrounds and how team members achieved their success. What we're talking about here is the relationship – a close relationship. I can't emphasize enough that this type of communication really must occur. Both parties engage each other so anything that needs to be ironed out in terms of a successful relationship is discussed.

In addition to all the process-oriented issues we talked about regarding onboarding a new team member, there is a basic premise in everything. Everybody comes into the business with a different view, a unique way of doing things. No two people are alike. One important characteristic that should be discussed is the fundamental concept called **patience.**

Each team member must exert a certain amount of patience for teams to have the success they want and need to have. Patience is critical because there are growing pains associated with onboarding a new team member.

Lest we forget, teaming is about putting together people with complementary skills and capabilities that are driven by, or strategically aligned with, the same value proposition and mission.

A few last words to remember: It can take a long time to get onboarded. That doesn't mean that the team member isn't providing some functional capabilities to the team, but it takes some time. If this is done correctly, it's going to take six months to a year to really get this new team member sufficiently onboarded.

Checklist for Onboarding a New Team Member

This checklist assumes that most of the human resources new-hire paperwork has been completed. This checklist focuses on assimilating the new team member onto the team. This list is not exhaustive; however, it will provide a decent start to the process.

1. Discuss the team's business plan and strategy document with the new team member.
2. Assign a mentor.
3. Discuss delegation of duties and responsibilities.
4. Discuss any special training needs and what the team will do to assimilate the new team member.
5. Have each team member explain their role on the team.
6. Integrate the new member on the technology platform including the customer relationship management (CRM) application.
7. Order business cards and stationery.
8. Establish performance goals and measurement standards.
9. Discuss the new team member's participation on both client and prospect meetings.
10. Debrief the new team member after each client/ prospect meeting and provide feedback.
11. Set aside time each week for the new team member to pitch at least one core product or service utilized by the team for clients.

Team Challenge

Develop your team's checklist for onboarding a new team member.

NOTE

1. https://www.thebalance.com/onboarding-1918832.

CHAPTER 13

Team Dysfunction: The Elephant in the Room

"Great teams do not hold back with one another. They are unafraid to air their dirty laundry. They admit their mistakes, their weaknesses, and their concerns without fear of reprisal."

—Patrick Lencioni, best-selling author
of books on team management

One of the most significant factors impacting team success is having a strong leader. It's the team leader's responsibility to keep the team focused on its objectives and mission. In successful teams, team members share the glory and the fruits of everyone's contributions no matter how large or how small. This is important for team cohesiveness. In large organizations, if you review team performance distribution, it will look a lot like a bell-shaped curve. Fifteen percent of the performers will be at the top of the performance distribution, 15% will be at the bottom, and 70% will be in the middle. The top 15% often get the rewards and accolades while the 70% in the middle receive very little in the way of recognition and accolades. Usually, the 15% at the bottom are made to feel inadequate. It's been said that if you eliminate the bottom 15%, there will be a new bottom 15% in the distribution of performance. The key is to make everyone feel that their contributions matter. This holds true at the micro level when you consider the performance of each team member. To the extent that the leader inspires and makes each team member feel valued, team synergy and breakthroughs can occur.

Teams must work diligently to ensure that there is a fair and equitable distribution of the workload. We are reminded of an example of a team that wanted to hire someone to do all the prospecting, marketing, and client acquisition for the team. This type of model rarely works and leads to dysfunction and failure. Lack of clarity about the mission rears its ugly head in the form of lack of initiative by team members.

The culture we grew up in the 1970s and 1980s rewarded individual performance through special incentives, recognition clubs, and trips. There were no rewards for collaboration and helping cross-functional teams succeed. The focus was on "me first," then everyone else. What if all of this changed and individual team members woke up in the morning wishing for another team member's success or for another team's success? This is a dilemma that many teams and organizations face today. This is clearly a paradigm shift in the way we look to eliminate team dysfunction. We are talking about a cultural change that will require a leadership focus. A response of "we have always done it this way" should no longer be adequate. We believe that measured risk taking should be defined as a vital component of cultural change.

We are not suggesting in any way that teams abandon the pursuit of quality work and sacrifice a solid compliance posture. As teams debate the issues, it's equally as important to eliminate the feeling that someone must be victorious or a winner. Collaboration and the collective wisdom involved with the team's overcoming impediments to success is critical to progress on many fronts. If teams focus not only on the symptoms but also deal with the root causes, they can then eliminate many of the issues associated with team dysfunction.

Patrick Lencioni is an author of books on business management, particularly in relation to team management. He identifies five dysfunctions of a team[1]:

1. The absence of trust: Many of you may have had the experience when you were afraid to speak up or ask a question due to fear of retribution. I remember being at a high-level managers' meeting and a manager wanted clarification of an important concept. He asked his question and was immediately publicly chided and berated in front of the group by the senior level manager. The senior level manager then asked the group, "Are there any more questions?" The room was so silent you could hear a pin drop!

If someone had a clever idea, or a better way of doing things, or the opportunity to improve efficiency, or profitability, it wasn't going to take place at that meeting! As you could well understand, others in the group didn't trust they would be heard. As a leader of a team or a team member, you want to be listened to and be heard. You want to know that expressing a difference of opinion will not jeopardize one's career. Absence of trust impacts the sharing of critical information that can improve team performance and cohesiveness. At times, it's inaction and complacency that can sabotage team performance.

We stress Team Huddle sessions as well as a variety of team meetings. Are all members of your team able to freely express opinions? Are members able to freely express their vulnerabilities? Do you notice defensive behaviors by team members that are impediments to success? If so, the team may be struggling with issues of trust.

2. Fear of conflict: Fear of conflict impacts a team when there is no free-spirited debate about issues that impact team performance. Does the team allow the passionate discussion to rise to the level where there is conversation on what to change, what to improve in terms of processes, the client experience, and team members sharing accountabilities and responsibilities? Team morale is negatively impacted when conflict isn't brought to the surface and discussed. Sometimes this is so severe that team members "vote with their feet" – they leave the team for a better opportunity. As a result, team members may even leave their firms and go to a competitor.

We have witnessed team conflicts emerge around compensation splits, delegation of duties and responsibilities, team members taking excessive time off, or a lack of accountability to goals. This is not an exhaustive list; however, these are some of the common sources of team conflict.

It's important for a team to set the ground rules or boundaries for challenging conversation for team members to get rid of the impediments to growth. The avoidance of team conflict can give team members a false sense of harmony when, in fact, the opposite is true. There should always be room for contentious discussion as long as mutual respect for everyone's feelings are observed.

3. Lack of commitment: The team has its weekly team meeting and decisions have been made; however, the following week the results are reviewed and they are less than desired. The team is "nodding" its head in agreement, but the team has no buy-in and clearly demonstrates a lack of commitment or accountability. Under close examination, you may find that the team doesn't have the skills or the training. Or perhaps team members don't feel their contributions matter. Whatever the issues are, the team must discuss the level of commitment and accountability to the project or goal. Sometimes, there may be a lack of strategic alignment between the actions that team members must take with their values or overall vision of the team. Each team member should feel that everyone has a voice that can be heard even if you can't always achieve a consensus view on every action item. Sometimes coming to work late and not being fully engaged in team functions, processes, and rituals can be interpreted as a lack of commitment or respect for the other team members. The result is dissatisfaction and conflict among team members.

4. Avoidance of accountability: If there is no accountability for performance goals and targets, there can be no perception of failure. The team falls into the comfort zone. Most people do not like to fail, which, in the case of financial advisors, is obtaining the desired business growth or meeting expectations for performance. It has often been said, "That which gets measured gets accomplished." If failure is treated with positive feedback and there is active discussion about the gaps in performance, what can be improved on, or how the team can make improvements and recommend alternative courses of action, then failure can be handled in a constructive manner. It becomes a learning experience. We recommend that teams should meet weekly to review their performance targets. The team may decide that specific performance targets are unrealistic either on the low end or on the high end.

5. Inattention to results: When the team wins, everyone wins! A team is only as good as the sum of its individual parts. Everyone contributes and everyone should participate in the team's overall success. The perfect storm for teams occurs when there is no strategic alignment around vision, strategy, values, purpose, and goals. Performance criteria hasn't been established, and compensation, rewards, and recognition are not tied to team results.

This is a lot like running the 440-yard dash in track. If a performance goal isn't established and your time is not being measured, how do you know if you have accomplished your goal? How can you create the practice regimen necessary for improvement?

While it's important to discuss their results, it is equally important for teams to take time out to "smell the roses" and celebrate success.

Avoidance of Groupthink

When each team member is aligned with the strategy and direction of the team, complacency can occur. Everyone is comfortable and self-assured. Seemingly, there are no conflicts. Almost all the team's activities are very predictable and creativity is somewhat muted. No member of the team is challenging process, marketing, or bringing any innovative ideas to the table. The team is in a rut and performance is starting to diminish. How does a team break out of this complacency to be able to continue to grow and be energized? The team must move from inward thinking to outward thinking.

Teams can schedule a joint meeting with another team outside of their market area for an idea exchange. Teams can discuss their business structures, prospecting methods, client service models, niche markets, and acquiring ultra-high-net-worth clients, for example. This works best when teams create specific agendas around these topics. Teams can hire a coach to work with them to develop innovative ideas.

An exchange of ideas around team successes and break-throughs are also helpful. If a team is currently doing $2.5 million in annual revenues, they should meet with a team doing between $5 and $7 million in revenues. The purpose of meetings of this nature is to brainstorm ideas and get an understanding of some of the best practices that have allowed these teams to obtain their specific performance breakthroughs. Sometimes seeing is believing and meeting with another team might provide inspiration that new breakthroughs can still occur.

Teams can schedule time with an asset manager to obtain innovative ideas and concepts that might be beneficial to clients. If the team has a specific weakness on an aspect of technology that can improve the business, the team should schedule a learning session.

Sometimes teams need some inspiration and motivation that can be fulfilled by going to a workshop. When teams take some time and challenge current ways of doing things and challenge their thinking, real breakthroughs are possible.

Additionally, teams can embark on a client feedback process and ask clients a variety of questions to collect information as to how the team is performing on key strategies. Some questions are:

- How can we improve our service delivery?
- Are there any gaps or needs that are not being met by our team?
- Is the team communicating with you in a timely manner?
- Are there some topical areas around retirement or lending that you would like to hear more about?
- In what areas of expertise that we currently provide are you most satisfied with?

While this list is not exhaustive, you are providing the opportunity for the client to give the team important feedback on service and performance.

How can we improve our service delivery? First, the client's expectations must be met in terms of the frequency of communication, the structure of the communication, client reviews, and doing the deep dive on problem areas and solutions. The key is making the client satisfied. Get that feedback from the client so that you can reinforce what the team is doing well and then begin to make some behavioral changes about the things that the team needs to improve that will be beneficial to the client experience.

We find that teams may have a functional expertise in a certain area, such as asset management, identifying appropriate money managers, or planning; however, there may be areas that the team is just not proficient in like tax minimization strategies, or working in the philanthropic niche with nonprofit boards. The team may decide that it has many opportunities in the nonprofit arena so they need to recruit someone to the team with that expertise or possibly collaborate with another team that has that level of expertise. (See more information in Chapter 7, "Team Collaboration.")

But keep in mind the cultural dynamic really started with teams or individuals being very protective of their turf as well as being very competitive and measuring performance against other team members or other financial advisors in an office environment. Sometimes these internal rankings and comparisons can be destructive, resulting in no one wanting to share experiences that might provide a competitive advantage or recognition to another advisor. The team must change again the paradigm that we talked about earlier if collaboration is going to take place.

Frequency of Client Communication

Our next question about the team communicating with the client in a timely manner means the frequency, of course. This is a crucial area. In other words, there could be events that change during a relationship. The client might be moving, or they have new grandchildren, or are taking care of an elderly parent. There could be a job change which points to 401(k) or retirement planning issues. There could also be the sale of a business that takes place. If the frequency of communication isn't timely, there could be many missed opportunities to provide service to the client. I'm reminded of the story of the client who sold a business for $5 million. The lack of communication between the current advisor and the client resulted in the assets being captured by another advisor and firm.

Whatever the circumstances are, it's good to know when significant changes are occurring in clients' lives so you can be there for them – not just to get more assets and potential revenues, but to be available as a support mechanism. It will clearly demonstrate that your motive in a relationship really is all about the client and taking care of them, not necessarily about the opportunity you may have to receive a fee. You need to believe that if you are not communicating with your clients in a timely manner, there are other competitors who will. They are trying to communicate with your clients through regular media, through social media, referral channels, and digital channels. Rest assured that attempts are being made to communicate with your clients by any number of competitive threats in the marketplace.

And don't forget: Communication is not just with the decision maker in the household. It may be with the spouse. It may be with adult children that, ultimately, might inherit the assets of the parent. Or there could be the potential for a windfall that the client might receive (i.e., an inheritance or a bonus from a new job). The frequency of communication and how you communicate with those clients becomes extremely important.

The fourth question about topical areas around retirement, or even lending, that the client would like to hear more about requires thinking about circumstances and how they change. Basically, you are doing continuous "profiling" of the client. You discover opportunities to do more business based on providing solutions to clients' problems. Some of the solutions offered might be in credit, lending, retirement, or long-term care. But if they don't know your team is conversant in these areas, they may not be initiated by the client.

And they can leave themselves vulnerable to a lender or another financial services institution, for example, and create a potential threat of another advisor gaining a foothold in a household relationship you manage. If you are looking at a lending or a credit opportunity, you list your assets – you almost must give up your "first born" on an application! And that's giving another institution an opportunity to gain a share of wallet by approaching your client relationships with ideas and concepts that you have not raised.

A question that is not asked of clients often enough is, "What areas of expertise that we currently provide are you most satisfied with?" The basis of this question is that there are things the team is doing very well that a client might value. And it's important that team members clearly understand this as they continue to shape and evolve their value propositions. When teams are focused on client acquisition and a client asks, "What value do you provide?," they can say, "Our clients have indicated to us that we provide an excellent value in managing risk, reducing tax liability, and providing eldercare solutions." Therefore, you want to be able to feed that back to your prospects. You also want to use that value-add and ask the client, "Are there individuals you know who can appreciate the value that we provide, and are you willing to make a personal introduction?" It's this enthusiastic endorsement you are seeking that can lead to referral opportunities.

When teaming and collaboration works well in organizations, we witness high morale, enthusiasm, sharing of ideas, performance enhancement, and environments where people are excited to come to work. Teams are a microcosm of the broader organizations they work for. The organizations that get this right will provide economic value added and increased shareholder value, and create sustainable organizations capable of handling disruptive threats in the marketplace.

Team Challenge

Develop some survey questions to ask clients in person. Schedule a meeting and have each team member discuss the findings, potential solutions, and areas for improvement. Spend time reviewing and clarifying the brief team assessment (see Table 13.1). Then discuss these items and appropriate solutions among yourselves, manager, or business coach.

(continued)

(*continued*)

Table 13.1 Team assessment

Five Dysfunctions	Strongly agree	Agree	Somewhat agree	A key problem area for the team
1. Absence of trust				
2. Fear of conflict				
3. Lack of commitment				
4. Avoidance of accountability				
5. Inattention to results				

NOTE

1. Patrick M. Lencioni, *The Five Dysfunctions of a Team: A Leadership Fable* (New York: John Wiley & Sons, 2002).

CHAPTER

14

The Leader/Manager Role
in Building and Coaching Teams

"Teamwork makes the dream work, but a vision becomes a nightmare when the leader has a big dream and a bad team."

—John C. Maxwell

It's our belief that managers are an undervalued resource; they're the unsung heroes – they move advisors toward a vision for success as well as helping them with their development. The manager leader must create the right environment in which teams can thrive. Without leadership, it's going to be very hard for teams to thrive. The right environment is created through building a culture that is sustainable. In other words, the leader must be fully engaged with the advisor teams.

We see the leader as your business strategist and coach. The manager as coach facilitates the building, creation, and leading of advisor teams. This is an individual who helps to promote collaboration among teams, both internally and across organizational silos. The leader is establishing a common vision among all the advisor teams in the market area of responsibility, and the vision is a unifying purpose among all the advisors. As a business strategist and coach, he or she meets with advisor teams at least on a quarterly basis and helps to shape business plans that meet the objectives of client, the advisor, and firm.

When you think about this role and how busy this individual is, it seems overwhelming. The leader must create an infrastructure in the office and build his or her internal team to be able to help execute on the advisors' most important activities that are necessary for success. We have witnessed some leaders having one or two sales managers, having individuals work with the onboarding of new advisors and establishing roles around administration, compliance, strategic marketing, and product areas and the tactical product areas for the firm.

The leader is the unifying person who helps elevate the entire team to have an impact on advisors. He or she understands the "pain points" in his market. For example, someone working in a Florida market might have a distinct set of pain points relative to retirees or opportunities as opposed to someone who might be working in a very entrepreneurial environment in the Silicon Valley in California. This is an individual who is going to understand their market and is diligent in helping and coaching advisors to seek out specialized niche markets and other business opportunities that might exist.

He or she can build and extend partnering relationships throughout the organization. There may be an area of expertise that doesn't exist within the branch, and it's up to the branch leader to examine the organization and create collaborative partnering opportunities. They may be with compliance, with marketing, with product groups, and they may be with specialists. They also may be with highly specialized divisions within the organization, whether institutional relationships or specialized retirement planning groups.

He or she is effective at building a team that supports the team-based environment with administrative staff, sales managers, product/market coordinators, and other advisor teams. This is an individual who leads through observation and interaction and asks questions to gain knowledge and information as to how best to provide support of the advisors within their branch.

This is a two-way street. While we are focused on managers, advisors need to challenge them to get certain things done that benefit the entire office and the advisor team. When this leader is out recruiting, he or she should ask a fundamental question to each advisor they try to onboard which is, "How are you being coached?" Recruits should ask the question, "How do you coach and lead your advisors?" For recruits who want to grow, that is a very important question. It speaks to your future growth potential through an offer of coaching and guidance.

It bears repeating: **These manager/leaders should ask the advisors they're trying to recruit how they're currently being coached.** The role of the manager and coach is often undervalued in terms of the impact that these leaders can have on building sustainable environments and impacting the communities they serve. When firms engage in frequent reorganizations and relocations, it can impact a leader's ability to have a long-term positive impact on their advisors. As a result, advisors can become cynical due to leadership change.

And if advisors are not being coached, what is the answer? If you really think about why are they not being coached, the face-to-face meetings with the advisor must be front and center, and how they delegate certain duties and responsibilities must be examined so that these manager/leaders can maximize the opportunity and time spent with them.

So why coach advisor teams? If you're really looking at trying to extract maximum organic growth out of an organization, helping teams become more successful is a key component of this strategy. These leaders can take several steps to remedy problems with team dynamics. The first is to work with teams to develop a common objective understanding of why team members are not collaborating effectively. Managers must examine these teams through interviews, evaluations, coaching, and reviewing advisor business plans. It's a substantial commitment of time, but the rewards and psychic income that comes from coaching and developing others is personally gratifying.

These leaders are also responsible for helping to correct dysfunctional team dynamics, which means they must focus attention on interventions. As soon as managers begin to observe a level of dysfunction that can put a team into a crisis, the leader must intervene and potentially mediate conflict. As the saying goes, it's up to this leader to try to "manage the ripples because ripples become waves and waves have the potential to become tsunamis." This means problems have the potential to escalate beyond repair at times.

If leaders don't manage that risk, teams may break up or they vote with their feet and they move to another organization thinking that will solve the problems. Being interactive in this way is also part of an advisor retention strategy. If a manager is building organic growth, retaining advisors and reducing turnover is part of the equation for success.

Part of the dynamics is being able to express sensitivity, being able to express understanding, and being able to remind advisors that you are there to help them with their business. These are some of the necessary soft skills. Part of it is trying to get team members aligned to the broader vision and strategy and making sure that this leader communicates the organization's purpose.

Leaders must examine the team's alignment, how teams are organized, and how they collaborate. Show an interest in teams by reviewing team agendas and communicating and checking in regularly with teams to ensure they're working consistently and collectively on the vision and the strategy. These actions help to provide direction and focus. These are all elements of team-based coaching.

McKinsey and Company studied top teams in organizations, and they reported that only 30% of the time was spent in productive collaboration.[1] They identified some examples of how poor dynamics depressed performance. It is these soft skills that very often no one pays a lot of attention to, but they impact performance and the metrics.

One of the things that these manager/leaders must do at the formation stage is to help teams get it right by helping teams get the right people on the bus, establish priorities, avoid conflict and disruption, and get the training they need to succeed. The real task of this leader is to build and nurture other potential team members as leaders. It's this balance between the team's needing some objectives in how they manage themselves and the leader's stepping in only appropriately to help these teams succeed.

The leader is being confronted on a day-in, day-out basis by numerous people – clients, advisors, support staff, operations, administrative personnel, and product vendors – who want their time. The leader must constantly establish priorities and make sure that they're focused on the priority activities that are going to impact team performance and enhance the branch revenues. The coach, the manager, the leader, one and the same – it's that person's job to represent the values of the organization as powerfully and as charismatically as possible. It is these leaders that set the example in everything that they do.

In an interview with the *Harvard Business Review*, Jeff Immelt, then CEO of GE, was asked, "What does a leader do?" His response was, "Drive change and develop other leaders."[2] And yes, it's also important to nurture the other team members as leaders and to talk about curbing the egos. There are many soft skills that leaders must use to understand their teams' interpersonal relationships and how to weigh and manage conflict, as well as curb the egos of individuals that could be disruptive to the team. Team members must understand that no one is bigger than the team, and they all must make sacrifices for the group. Team leaders must set aside personal egos and remember they are working for the greater goal of helping the team succeed. It's a difficult soft skill that is required to diffuse conflict so that the team continues to move forward. This is a huge transformation for many team leaders.

The role of the manager/leader is multifaceted. These leaders must be adept at strategic planning and understanding the unique markets within their area of operations. They must lead advisors in embracing and understanding many of the changes that are occurring in a changing marketplace. The leader must adapt and organize their operations that support clients and advisors. This leader must establish controls for profitability as well as managing the compliance posture in their offices while managing risk.

This leader is also a business strategist who meets one-on-one with advisors to lead and ensure that there is alignment with the goals and vision of the company. A business strategist is responsible for determining the direction and scope of his office. The business leader is also a coach responsible for the development of his or her people. One of the keys to this coaching effort is mentoring and developing others who can assume leadership roles within the office. When this leader takes an interest in the personal development of others, these individuals will, in turn, reciprocate by offering their support in the offices as mentors and coaches for advisors within the office. If the leader is developing and fostering a collaborative culture, it will permeate throughout the entire office. These individuals can become a de-facto leadership team in the office and should be organized in a way that provides organized training and support for them as well as for teams in the office.

The role of these leaders has become so complex over the years that a collaborative team-based model must be utilized to leverage the capabilities of the leader, like the way an advisor team might operate with delegation of duties, responsibilities, and accountabilities. This leader is also a conductor when it comes time for mobilizing his or her teams. Sometimes, this leader might bring in a team either within his office or from another office and hold a developmental meeting for the sharing of ideas and concepts. These breakout sessions are designed to focus attention on the strategies necessary to enable teams to break new thresholds of performance.

The role of leader, as illustrated in Figure 14.1, is multifaceted and has a high degree of complexity if performed appropriately. Leaders must *plan* and *organize strategies* to have a positive impact on market penetration, client service, *coaching,*

Figure 14.1   Role of leader.

and training and development of all employees, as well as growing revenues. Metrics are generally handed down from above; however, you must provide *leadership* to accomplish firmwide goals while paying close attention to the unique attributes of your market or service area. These activities must be done while *controlling* costs and maintaining the compliance posture within your branch.

As a leader, you are the business strategist for your market. You are analyzing opportunities to have an enormous impact. While there are problems and issues that abound, you must stay vigilant and create strategies for success.

We have spent some time discussing the manager as leader/coach. Now let's examine a process as described in Figure 14.2 for managers to implement this seven-step process.

Step 1: The assessment/preparation: Before you bring in an advisor team for coaching, you must perform an assessment of the team. Gather all relevant reports and data on the team members. Examine the quantitative data and qualitative data for the team and team members. At a minimum, review revenue reports, household growth reports, product mix, financial plans, and plan implementation. Also, review client satisfaction reports, net new money, and annuitized business reports to name a few. We realize that these reports vary by firm. The point is that you want to understand as much about the team as you can prior to engaging them in the coaching and business strategist roles.

Step 2: Strategy: You want to communicate the vision and objectives for your office and firm. You are trying to establish congruence and alignment of the team's mission and goals with that of the organization. The time spent here is designed to make sure everyone is on the same page. Conduct a SWOT (strengths, weaknesses,

Figure 14.2 Seven-step coaching process.

opportunities, and threats) analysis as discussed in a previous chapter. Ask the advisor team for feedback. Is there alignment with firm strategy and the team?

Step 3: Gap analysis: In this step, the leader will discuss the gaps in alignment between the firm and the advisor. The leader should also discuss any challenges and problem areas that are in conflict between the two parties as well as where there is common ground. Identify opportunities and areas for improvement. What behavioral changes need to be discussed? (This is a joint effort between the manager and the advisor team.)

Step 4: Seek agreement: Confirm with the team the gaps that require special attention and focus.

Step 5: Discuss potential solutions: The solutions might be the best course of action, recommendations, and improvements to the practice. Are the recommended solutions realistic? Negotiate solutions between manager and advisor. It's important that these methods not be presented as dictum but rather as possibilities. Identify and discuss best-practice solutions.

Step 6: Create an action plan: Have the team create an action plan with initiatives, tasks, timing or timetable, and who will be responsible for the implementation. Prepare a joint written action plan with key initiatives, tasks, timing, and responsibilities. Establish measurable goals and critical next steps.

Step 7: Schedule sessions for monitoring and feedback: Sometimes, this is a meeting and, at times, a simple note written on a performance report with a green or blue felt-tip pen is enough. Providing a congratulatory word or words of encouragement indicate that you, as the leader, care about the team. Schedule checkups and inspect progress. Sessions should be scheduled three or four times per year. Characterize the sessions as business planning and strategy meetings. Calling them "reviews" has a negative connotation. Remember, you are engaging the advisor team in a coaching or developmental session.

Outcomes

If you are engaging your advisor teams in this manner, you will impact and create a culture of excellence in your office environment. You will foster communication and collaboration in the branch or office you have been chosen to lead. Your awareness of what needs to be done in your office will become clearer because you will be earning the trust of your advisors and team members, and they will be more inclined to share information with you. You will coach teams to higher levels of performance and show them the pathways to get to their destination.

Leader Challenge

Meet with your leadership team and develop your coaching model and vison for your team's future. Make sure that all advisor teams have a business plan that is not just constructed but is discussed with you several times per year. Utilize the coaching model as discussed in this chapter.

NOTES

1. www.mckinsey.com/business-functions/organization/our -insights/world-class-teams.
2. Steven Prokesch, "How GE Teaches Teams to Lead Change," *Harvard Business Review,* January 2009.

15

Wealth Management in the Digital Age

"New developments in machine intelligence will make us far smarter as a result, for everyone on the planet. It's because our smartphones are basically supercomputers."

—Eric Schmidt, Executive Chairman, Google, USA

The overarching trend that impacts financial advisors in a significant way is the disruptive change created by technology or digital strategies. The current generation of millennials has grown up with technology and is very comfortable using it. In fact, be careful they aren't the only ones embracing this transformation into a digital world. My 85-year-old mother is comfortable navigating the Internet and looking up recipes online. Transitioning to other Internet-based capabilities will not be a big challenge. More and more, we are all getting used to life with technology. We are using the Global Positioning System (GPS) in our autos, and our smartphones are loaded with a host of applications. We are measuring our exercise programs and using a tablet to replace our television remote controls. We have Wi-Fi throughout our homes to use our laptops and tablets. This evolution is not just about the "younger generation." The impact on financial advisors and the firms they work for is continuing to evolve at a rapid pace.

As soon as the latest technology is introduced, it becomes outdated within 18 months since innovation is taking place at such a rapid pace. The financial services industry is trying to stay ahead of the game; however, much of the innovation is taking place outside of the ecosystem of the major firms. This innovation is commonly referred to as "fin-tech" or financial services technology. Adoption of modern technologies centers around three important characteristics: An evolving regulatory environment, institutional inertia and the issue of legacy systems, and gaining the public's trust will be key to ensuring widespread adoption of new financial technologies.

A key trend that impacts financial advisors and teams in a significant way is the disruptive change created by the many technology or digital strategies. But before we get ahead of our-selves, let's examine a little history that points to the fact that this evolution is really taking place and how it might impact teams.

Some History

I entered the business in 1978, and the technology we used was called a Quotron machine. It was basically a desktop PC 286, and you couldn't do much with it. You could only extract infor-mation; you couldn't put information back into it other than simple account opening information. It was the first financial data technology to deliver stock market quotes to an electronic screen rather than on a printed ticker tape. We had rows of stocks that we followed that would flash to alert us if any price changes were occurring.

The competitive advantage that we had as a firm in those days was the way in which information was pushed to us in a very transactional world. Information was a specialty of the firms that provided it, whether it be research on various companies or fixed income; reports on almost every product area were pro-vided by research analysts in the firms that we worked for.

Much of the innovation occurred with new product devel-opment. By that I mean ideas like liquid yield option notes, zero coupon bonds, Tigers, Spyders (SPDRs), and now exchange-traded funds (ETFs). I remember the New Perspective mutual fund, which was one of the first mutual funds we had mar-keted. There were plenty of tax-sheltered products involving helicopter leasing, DNA plant technology, real estate, and thoroughbred horse racing, to name a few. Wall Street was being very innovative in all sorts of hybrid equity and fixed income products, and, as a firm, we would be the first to market these products to a constituency. We would always be the first to show investors something new, and that gave us a marketing edge or first mover advantage. Talking about something new, something exciting, generated a certain excitement out there in the public domain.

When we introduced the cash management account in the 1970s, the brokerage account as we knew it changed forever. It became a combination of the brokerage account and the money market account, and access to your information was a statement with which you had access to the money through a Visa debit card and a check-writing privilege. It took competitors 18 months to respond to that kind of creativity, disruption, and innovation. While the minimum account size was $20,000, very quickly the average account grew within a few years to over $275,000. This type of an account is a staple in most firms today.

The traditional money market account had maybe $5,000 or $10,000, and the idea was to use it as a "parking vehicle" in which, when a transaction occurred and needed to be paid, you'd debit the money market account and meet the payment obligation by settlement date usually in five days. What's been happening is that a lot of the innovation has been coming outside of Wall Street investment firms. This lock on capturing all the creativity of these brilliant minds, from a technology point of view, isn't necessarily with those firms.

When you think about disruption, innovation, and sustainability, the question remains: "Is Wall Street going to try to take advantage of technology once it is created, or will it to try to create or develop its own disruption in the marketplace to gain a competitive advantage?"

We believe firms must be able to manage the client relationships and the data mining of client information. This will have the potential to give firms more precise information about their clients, their spending habits, lifestyles, charities, and more. In the past, we viewed client connectivity based on their having five or six services. We might have their mortgage, their cash management account, a managed solution, a portfolio of professional asset managers, and their retirement plan or individual retirement account (IRA). You might do a financial plan for that client or some insurance, or a liability management product (credit and lending). That created what we called "stickiness" with the client, which made it very difficult for the client to leave the advisor because they were attached to all these different services that were provided. Most products and research available today is a commodity, meaning that there is no longer a differentiating competitive advantage. Every firm has a similar offering. This is the environment that teams face today. How will teams differentiate themselves in a commoditized marketplace with continuous pressure on fees being charged?

Now, as we started to look at the future, how will advisor teams and firms create an improved connectivity with clients. We are seeing clients connecting with their banks online and using mobile technologies. Automated bill payment services have been around for quite some time. Perhaps differentiated applications that connect clients directly to their advisors at specific scheduled times in an automated way are close at hand. If a firm has its own competitive applications that provide two-way connectivity, perhaps artificial intelligence will be used for the basic questions and responses. The more ways in which firms can connect and provide useful services to clients via technology will be a differentiating competitive advantage in the foreseeable future. The extent to which firms begin to look at ways to understand the opportunity and connect with their client in multiple ways will be an important retention strategy, which means you might send a YouTube video link on a product or service or something that's interesting that they might want to hear about.

You might communicate with them via Skype or other two-way video technology services, which allows clients to basically have a face-to-face meeting with you even though they're not sitting in your office. We don't know how we're going to use all this technology at this point. But one of the things that we do know is that small industry players are going in and capturing market share. For example, when you look . at firms like Betterment, Wealthfront, Personal Capital, Motif, and other digital advice channels, they're getting a toehold in consumer relationships. It begs the question: How will advisors take advice and guidance and couple technology and provide a unique client experience? Advisors will need to anchor the client relationship in a way that marries high tech, but with a high-touch capability going forward.

What About the Teams?

I'm reluctant to talk about the technology that can be used today because it may very well become passé in 18 months, as I mentioned at the beginning of the chapter. But how are teams using technology? They are using it for everything from customer relationship management (CRM) tools to access client information to applications that help manage workflows, applications that help with portfolio management and rebalancing, account aggregation, and other client management capabilities. There are tools that enable alerts to take place when it's time to talk to a client and to recall what the previous conversation was about; overall client communication digitally, face-to-face via the client's mobile or iPad, no matter where the client might reside; and all the social media connections like LinkedIn, for example, using it to cross-check whom the client might have affiliations with, which might lead to referral opportunities.

There are online calculators that do a ton of analyses and tablet computers for showing client presentations. These tools are becoming very easy for clients to use and calculate their own "what if" scenarios for retirement planning, lending, or credit decisions. There are CRM tools, and advisors now have websites. They just need to be marshaled to the point where they're able not to just create information but also to use a funneling process by which these sites can generate leads. When teams look at what's out there, what's available to make their lives easier, but also to look at how they establish more and more connectivity with the client, that becomes the idea around the use of technology.

And look at the potential for virtual teammates, where there may be a team member with a specialized expertise or capability who might be domiciled in another location or state and can connect to the team via a technology. The challenge for advisor teams is to be familiar with these capabilities, use them, and to be sure to have permission via the compliance department within the firms. We believe that you can't begin to fully tap the potential creative use of technology until you start exploring how to use it to your best advantage. If you take the concepts of collaboration and you use technology as an enabler, you can use the Force Multiplier Effect to make sure that you're managing external relationships as well. That could be a true force multiplier and enhance collaboration among teams and make them more effective.

As the creation and development of one-off technologies continues, how can these innovations be packaged into one comprehensive solution that is compatible with all of them? Going to one application and inputting data in a CRM, and then entering similar information across a broad range of client solutions such as cash management, a financial plan, a retirement account, or a mortgage application, is time consuming and detracts from client-facing activities by the team members. Most advisors we speak with would prefer to enter information/data once and have it available for multiple applications. Instead, information about the client must be entered on multiple platforms. This creates an inefficient use of time.

If the team is going after niche markets, they should be able to go online and pull research, publications, and other data within their targeted market area. Technology should help the team source this data and assimilate marketing content to target these specific groups. The data is already in the public domain. Next, the team might want to mine data about any client that is prominent within that specialized niche market and identify via social media for referral opportunities.

Millennials have surpassed Baby Boomers as the nation's largest living generation, according to population estimates released by the US Census Bureau. Millennials, whom we define as those ages 18 to 34 in 2015, now number 75.4 million, surpassing the 74.9 million Baby Boomers (ages 51 to 69). And Generation X (ages 35 to 50 in 2015) is projected to pass the Boomers in population by 2028.[1]

Teams will need to think about strategies to bring on and capture some of these tech-savvy Millennials who are comfortable using technology. Teams will need to add a Millennial team member to perhaps understand and communicate with this demographic. There is a risk that if assets transfer from the Baby Boomer generation to this demographic and advisors don't have relationships with these heirs, they risk losing assets to perhaps a digital advice wealth management channel.

There are more than 80 million Millennials in the United States with an aggregate net worth of more than $2 trillion; by 2018, that is expected to grow to $7 trillion.[2]

In summary, these are the top industry trends we see having an impact.

Technology/Digital Capabilities

Potential customers have access to the same information as advisors in real time. They can go online or use mobile technologies which gives them information any time, any place and anywhere. This is why information is such a commodity.

Rise of Team-Based Advisors

For the sole practitioner, access to information, as well as the expansion of the number of products and services and the ever-increasing demands of the client base, is taxing and puts pressure on client service. Teams that carve out specialties among each team member to do a deeper dive with clients will become vital to continued success.

Emergence of Nontraditional Competitors

It seems everyone is in the lucrative financial services business. It's hard to distinguish the difference between banks, brokerages, insurance companies, and discount providers. Now you have firms like Betterment, Wealthfront, and Motif, to name a few firms that are attracting customers online doing basket trades at $9.95 or charging 25 basis points for services. These firms create disruption in the marketplace. Everyone is competing for a share of the consumer's wallet. Deep discounting is taking on a whole new meaning. This places pressure on the incumbent firm's ability to raise prices. The rise of digital advice platforms with price transparency that provide direct-to-the-consumer models for investment advice are on the rise and offer scalability to underserved markets.

Outsourcing and Open Architecture

More and more servers rest in the cloud rather than on the premises of many firms. The ability to rent server space, host websites, and access products and services is creating efficiency and allowing advisors in the independent channel to have the same or similar tools as the large wirehouse firms. They are also becoming agile and able to respond to technological innovation. Firms like Envestnet, FOLIOfn, Trust Company of America, and Pershing provide not only custody capabilities but also product and service capabilities. These firms are providing gateways or access points for advisors and their firms that didn't exist before.

Differentiation and Applied Intelligence

Set yourself apart by applying your communications abilities, analytical skills, and collective wisdom to the benefit of your clients and being able to comprehensively deliver more than a commodity client experience. It's the value-added capability that an advisor can provide that justifies the fees being charged. This is a substantial client benefit that should not be overlooked.

Mass Commoditization of Products and Research

There was a time when a firm could innovate a new product and it took the competition 18 months to two years to respond with something similar. The Internet and technology allow a firm to replicate the same product within days of its competitors. Research is no longer proprietary; it's everywhere.

Pursuit of Multiple Channels of Business Development

Advisors will need to proactively create alliances with centers of influence and strategic partners. They will need to establish niche markets and become experts in those markets. They will need to be adept at using social media (i.e., LinkedIn for references and business development). Understanding who a client is connected to in terms of interconnected relationships is key to gaining substantial referral opportunities.

Rising Customer Expectations Due to the Internet

Because of the Internet providing access to financial information, customers will ask, "What am I getting from my advisor?" Teams will need to have a response and a unique value proposition. Teams will need to be efficient in delivering their capabilities and service. New fee models will need to be created because of continued price compression on products and services.

Data Mining

Utilizing account aggregation services (Morningstar's By All Accounts) gives you a complete picture of where your clients' assets are and their spending. This access to data will allow you to improve efficiency in delivering client solutions. CRM tools can provide data, analytics, sales pipeline management, and the generation of advisor and client reports from the cloud. We must get to a point where data about the client resides in the cloud, which is useful in establishing multiple accounts without multiple data entry points.

An Expanding Wealth Management Market

According to research, the future possibilities in the use of technology on the horizon are a "larger [or expanding] wealth management market serving clients across multiple segments (from mass market to ultra-high net worth) through fully automated solutions, [and with] traditional high-touch advisors, and hybrid versions of the two that combine virtual advisor interaction with automation and self-service technology-based tools."[3]

Artificial Intelligence

Can machines think like humans? Artificial intelligence (AI) is having machines perform a variety of tasks, including reasoning, planning, learning, and understanding language. The use of this technology is designed to create greater efficiency and make our jobs easier. The advancement in this technology is possible due to the increase in computer processing power. There has been a trillion-fold increase in computation power over the past 60 years. We now take it for granted when we speak into our smartphones to look up phone numbers, ask for directions, and find research information. It recognizes our voice and acts accordingly. Firms like SalesForce.com are already researching and exploring AI concepts to change how people interface with clients.

We believe we are in for a ride as technology will continue to have an enormous impact on the financial services industry in the years ahead. Firms and advisor teams will have no choice but to embrace the change and think thoughtfully how to use innovation as a force multiplier to positively impact the client experience.

Team Challenge

Conduct a team meeting and discuss the use of technology. Are there areas within the team business model where technology can be used to streamline the business? Are there improvements to client service that can be made using technology? Is there some specialized training to sharpen the team's skill set on the use of technology? Who on the team will take the lead in identifying the team's priorities on the use of technology?

NOTES

1. http://www.pewresearch.org/fact-tank/2016/04/25/millennials -overtake-baby-boomers/.
2. https://blog.wealthfront.com/one-billion-assets-under-manage ment/.
3. www.ey.com/Publication/vwLUAssets/Advice_goes_virtual_in _asset_management/$FILE/ey-digital-investment-services.pdf.

CHAPTER 16

Diverse Teams and Niche Markets

"Strengths lie in differences, not in similarities."

—Stephen R. Covey

There is a compelling case to be made for the formation, development, and leadership of diverse teams. Considering the global trends; tough competition; more complex regulatory environment; and cross-border, cross-cultural geographic dispersed operations, there becomes a need to think about diverse teams in a unique way. Diverse teams must become more of "the norm" at all levels of organizations. Diversity can be defined as anything that isn't homogeneous – gender, age, nationality, ethnicity, sexual orientation, religion, or cultural groups. It can even include physical disabilities.[1]

Some of the teams may have members who have joined and have had an opportunity to learn a language, or may even have some international experience. Education, industry, and work experience all contribute to the different perspectives that can help engage teams as they look to grow market share in various parts of the country and the world. I live in the San Francisco Bay area. More than 112 different languages are spoken here, and 45% of all San Francisco residents do not speak English at home.[2]

Much of the research shows that diversity results in better performance.[3] When people of diverse backgrounds approach complex decisions, they can approach a problem from a variety of experiences – and especially when you look at the challenges that are faced by global firms. Diversity has an enormous impact on organizations that are undertaking broader and new initiatives and technology, and diversity of the team is very important for execution.

You might be thinking strategically and globally but acting locally in terms of where you might be domiciled as a team. However, you want an organization that has an agility to allow these teams to move across cultural, geographic, and functional business units that support the needs of the broader organizations.

A lot of diversity thought leadership in the past has been about balancing a homogeneous group for all to be thinking the same way. Now we've found that tension is created when there are differences. Teams need to be coached on how to be accepting of different views that can be combined to solve major problems or make decisions, as opposed to just looking at a single viewpoint where the outcome is only going to be as good as one person's thinking.

Insight from a Diversity Expert

We spent time discussing diversity and its challenges with Ronald B. Brown, PhD, President, Banks Brown. Dr. Brown is an expert and innovator in the fields of leadership development, diversity, and inclusion and organizational change. He consults with Fortune 100 corporations, and his experience spans more than 30 years.[4] To begin our discussions with Dr. Brown, we wanted to better understand: How do we get people (teams) to move forward beyond the differences associated with getting people of diverse backgrounds to work together and experience the benefits of the tension that is created because of diversity?

According to Dr. Brown, teams and leaders inside organizations must frame the tension that is created as an asset that provides a sort of dynamic creative energy that can bring a diverse way of looking at problems and arriving at solutions. In multicultural environments, we must acknowledge and value differences in thought and problem-solving approaches. When a team or organization solely values the predictability of all team members, options and creativity are also limited. For instance, improvisations by a diverse team member could be interpreted as differing from the norm in the way the team has habitually operated in the past. Therefore, misunderstandings regarding differences can lead to reluctance to embrace change, such as adopting new strategies, establishing niche markets, or reimagining the vision or mission of the team.

Leadership must invite discovery and deep reflection as well as be introspective about the viewpoints of all team members. The key takeaway is to seek true understanding to enable all team members to feel valued. Dr. Brown views all team members as assets that bring different strengths and capabilities to the team. How a team values these different mind-sets and motivations can lead to a range of solutions and possibilities to manage any potential conflict.

Rigid adherence to a set approach can stymie creativity on teams and lead to deficit assumptions that the diverse team is not approaching the problem in "the right way." Diverse teams with cross-functional team members have the potential to integrate different thoughts and experiences. Senior management in support of teams must break down organizational silos that create impediments to team success. From a multicultural perspective, leadership must prepare and create environments for diverse teams to thrive. When this element of cultural awareness occurs, real discovery can take place, which adds to an improved client experience.

If you are going to really leverage a diverse group, as well as the energy and synergy that they bring, then to not take advantage of this potential is a huge failure point. These diverse teams, because of their differences, must eliminate any barriers to communication when they're involved in the engagement with the team or project. Trying to help or move the diverse team toward mutual understanding might take more time and effort, so it's important for teams to not get frustrated by this tension created and negate the opportunity associated with the kind of teamwork that diverse teams can bring to the table. Diverse teams should be bringing more of a global mind-set and openness to the organization. When you even think about the market capitalization that lies outside the United States, having diversity can help shape the success of many organizations.

Women as a High-growth Market

Look at the demographic case about wealth being created in many diverse markets and subsets of diverse markets – meaning women, ethnic minorities, and individuals of different genders that also provide a variety of different experiences. Research[5] has been conducted about how the financial services industry could risk missing trillions of dollars in potential business in the United States simply because its professionals aren't really thinking about the behaviors that are needed to approach these diverse cultures and different markets. Let's just take the market for women investors as an example. Women control and influence over $11.2 trillion in the United States alone. That's 39% of the nation's investible assets. How teams and firms approach women becomes very critical. A firm messaging to women and an understanding of their consumer behavior becomes critical to success. Women, like other investors, want to meet their financial goals. But there are some differences in how they go about it.

One cultural difference among women investors is their need and desire to support the communities in which they reside. If an advisor is approaching prospective women investors, that's just one of many characteristics that they need to understand that could impact that relationship – understanding women, understanding their needs, their sensitivities, and the various approaches so that a homogeneous team doesn't just take a condescending approach to women. This is an example of why you really need to understand diverse markets.

Other research was also done on women in the United States, the United Kingdom, India, China, Hong Kong, and Singapore. They looked at women who had annual incomes of at least $100,000 or investible assets of $500,000 or more, and the research indicated that more than half – 53% of these women – don't have financial advisors; and in the United States 46% of women wealth creators and 75% of women under 40 were reporting they didn't have an advisor. When you think about niche markets, think about trying to reach a subset of the population. The numbers are enormous, and teams and firms can't afford to concede this business to other providers. It represents an opportunity cost lost to wealth management firms that don't pay attention to those demographics. It's estimated that the US wealth management firms might be leaving $5 trillion of assets on the table. (We talk more about niche markets later in this chapter in the Narrow Your Focus section.) Also, about 40% of the women say they don't feel understood by their advisor, and that's a major market failing point.[6]

The Wisdom Case

According to the *Harvard Business Review,* a body of research[7] revealed some additional benefits of workplace diversity. They discovered that these nonhomogenous teams are simply smarter in their approach to problems and challenges. And when we say smarter, they're really looking at collective wisdom that is provided to clients.

Putting together the collective wisdom of individuals seeing business issues differently and thinking about business issues differently takes courage. When teams from diverse backgrounds collaborate cross-functionally, they become aware of their own biases, and the fact-entrenched ways of thinking must be overcome. It might overshadow their ability to see solutions to problems because of their desires. And when you bring teams together to conquer preconceived notions about solving a problem, remarkable things can happen as a result, and fewer errors occur in the decision-making process.

There is always a challenge when a team onboards a member who has a unique perspective. The initial reaction from team members might be, "We want people who think like us. We don't want people to challenge our thinking." But when you allow the engagement to take place, the payoffs can be significant.

Research also shows that diverse teams bring a certain level of innovation to their firms. We're in an environment where businesses are continuously being disrupted, so how do you bring this diverse thought to the table, to the conference room, to the boardroom? Focus on how organizations can look at their capacity for change, making transformations, thinking thought-fully about their products, and hiring women and culturally diverse team members. The research will reveal that companies with more women, for example, are more likely to introduce radical new innovations into the market over a period.[8]

We believe that teams must look like our society at large, so we can't pretend that people with disabilities and diverse cultures and ethnicities don't exist. It's the differences that makes us great, and the same principles should be applied to the workplace. If you're hiring people who don't look, talk, or think like you do, and you create an environment where everybody must be singular in terms of their thinking, creativity will be stifled, and that will discourage innovation.

When you begin thinking about creating a diverse workplace, you want team members to question their assumptions and biases as well as open their minds to looking and seeing different points of view. When teams do that, they are creating practices that allow team members to feel they have a voice and are being heard. This openness will help to make the team smarter and, ultimately, help to make organizations successful whatever the objectives or the goals might be.

Diversity Can Be a Competitive Differentiator

McKinsey and Company also conducted some research, and they found that companies in the top quartile for gender or racial and ethnic diversity were going to have financial returns above the national industry mediums.[9] The companies in the bottom quartile were statistically less likely to achieve above-average returns. Diversity then becomes a competitive differentiator, and it starts to shift market share toward diverse companies over time. Diversity can work to the benefit of advisory teams as well.

I was sitting on a board of a nonprofit, and the board was very diverse, including women, people with disabilities and different sexual orientation and gender. They had put their $10 million endowment out for a competitive bid to be managed. There were five well-known companies competing for the business, and they all came in with their pitch. All things being equal, they each had an approach that made sense. There was one team that came in that happened to be diverse. They seemed to relate better to a variety of the board members and, as a result, it was the board's comfort level with the diverse team that ultimately contributed to the team's winning the business. That's just an example that gave this diverse team a little bit of an extra edge in winning the $10 million endowment.

A Collaborative Case

We talked about the intelligence that these diverse teams bring to the table. The idea of collaborating with a different team that might understand a woman's perspective and insight may bring different experiences than a male perspective to the table – they can leverage that wisdom to bring these inclusive behaviors to bear on a client relationship and engender long-term relationships. We believe that some degree of conflict is okay if it doesn't get out of hand. Teams must work with differences of opinion and not shy away from the diverse perspectives that don't necessarily match their own. And when you do that, you start to build trust. In an age of innovation and disruption, frank discussions and questions about strategy and direction must take place – questions like, "Why do we have to do it this way? Why can't we go after new markets? Why don't we embrace this innovative technology?" And again, it's the soft skills of communication and diversity of opinion and thought that really will lead to impressive results. We've all experienced this dynamic tension that occurs in many of the environments in which we have worked. You don't want people to work in an environment characterized by constant tension. However, these tensions can be overcome.

People Development Is Key

This is how we move teams away from some of the old ways of thinking. It is about stepping outside your comfort zone and moving to where the magic happens. We can no longer operate with the premise of slinging enough mud against the wall and hoping some of it sticks – that's too risky for organizations to do because turnover is too costly. We believe you shouldn't just hire people; you should make sure there is a nurturing environment ready to accept and support them. This is where leadership can make a real difference. Sometimes, leadership places people in stretch assignments, then leaves them alone, absent any coaching – basically saying, "I'm washing my hands; I've fulfilled my duty and my obligation." Well, the duty and obligation doesn't end with merely hiring or putting somebody in the role. You really must take responsibility for people development.

The most important thing that can be done is to develop and mentor people at every level of the organization, and teams can't escape that either. The mentee has an obligation as well. The mentee must set aside mental baggage or potentially unfair treatment that might be characteristic of previous experiences, and make the extra effort to establish those working relationships with their peers, their bosses, and others. Who knows, someone may take an interest and mentor you.

And at the heart of diversity, there are differences. It's those differences that make us better. We see things differently and have different approaches to problems, and we find creative solutions.

Narrow Your Focus: Become a Big Fish in a Small Pond

Let's say that the focus of your team was to target attorneys as potential clients. Perhaps there was a specialized group of attorneys like estate planning attorneys, or those that work on personal injury cases – that's establishing specific niche markets. Niches do not exist; they are created by thinking about the needs, the wants, and what might be required, or what was being addressed poorly, and that creates opportunities for the team.

Niche marketing is aimed at trying to be a "big fish in a small pond" as opposed to just being a "small fish in this huge pond." What you're trying to do is narrow your focus into specific groups where you learn everything there is to know about a particular market, and what you can offer as a subject matter expert in the development of client relationships. There are also subsets of markets on which diverse advisor teams can focus their efforts. If you think about applying big-picture thinking about team diversity and think about agile advisor teams, we believe that the human dynamics still exist. And the challenge is that there are barriers that all teams face when conflict arises. Teams need ground rules and training to overcome the barriers that impede success and many of the dysfunctions that have previously been discussed.

Diverse teams sometimes suffer because we're all human and individuals struggle at times to understand, trust, and relate to people that have diverse backgrounds or perspectives. Relationships can become distressed due to differences; however, the gap of understanding creates both tension and opportunities. Unfortunately, sometimes sabotage rears its ugly head or the lack of cooperation or communication impacts progress, and it undermines people. The process when conflict does occur is that teams, with the help of either a coach or an intermediary, learn to reconcile the differences or consider alternative approaches so that the team can move toward a sophisticated understanding and exploration of ideas.

Diverse teams can also be a great benefit because team members possess different perspectives and a wider variety of information. The process of reconciling these differences leads to deeper consideration of issues, more sophisticated understanding, and broader exploration of ideas, all of which boost performance.[10]

According to the research, adding a team member from a different department in the company or even one who grew up in a different state may add just enough of a difference to improve group performance.

How do you bring people from diverse backgrounds together? One answer is to think about bringing them together socially. This sounds basic, but it works. When you bring people together socially, you begin to break down the barriers that keep people apart. Some examples that might work for your team include:

- Baseball game and barbecue; divide the group into teams.
- Karaoke night; create unlikely pairings for duets.
- Bowling night; create teams or team challenges.
- Cinco de Mayo party or a similar themed party.
- A night at the theater.

These are just a few examples that worked for me. Fun is the perfect recipe for establishing team cohesiveness. We are not suggesting that having a few social activities solves the problem when team members have deep-seated wounds. Bringing in an experienced facilitator to help with the process of improvement might be in the team's best interest or possible 360-degree feedback sessions, if positioned appropriately.

Team Challenge

The team should discuss the onboarding of team members with diversity of opinions and thoughts. The team should assess whether all team members are fully engaged in discussions that can elevate team performance. Be frank and ask the team, "Are we inclusive and embracing differences"? Organize a nonwork fun activity for the team outside the work environment.

NOTES

1. http://lexicon.ft.com/Term?term=diverse-teams.
2. http://www.sfgate.com/bayarea/article/BAY-AREA-Report-112 -languages-spoken-in-2692403.php.
3. http://www.mckinsey.com/business-functions/organization/our -insights/why-diversity-matters.
4. http://banksbrownstrategy.com/index.php.
5. https://hbr.org/2014/12/the-financial-services-industrys -untapped-market.

6. https://hbr.org/2014/12/the-financial-services-industrys -untapped-market.

7. https://hbr.org/2016/11/why-diverse-teams-are-smarter.

8. https://www.psychologytoday.com/blog/your-brain-work/ 201703/why-diverse-teams-are-smarter.

9. http://www.mckinsey.com/business-functions/organization/our -insights/why-diversity-matters.

10. https://www.cluteinstitute.com/ojs/index.php/JDM/article/ viewFile/4966/5058.

17

Team Summary

"Great teamwork is the only way we create the breakthroughs that define our careers."

—Pat Riley

I t is crucial to reinforce the team's expectations for itself and its clients. False expectations and lack of belief in the team strategy is a major failure point. It leads to team dysfunction. Teams need to be reminded, "Why did we form a team? Why do we exist in the first place?" Here are a few reasons why the team exists, and following the list are detailed explanations:

- Deliver the promise and value proposition.
- Improve the quality of life for every team member.
- Provide value to your customers and enhanced service.
- Succession strategies for a team member exit/retirement from the business.
- Productivity improvement through team leverage.
- Growing the business through client retention and acquisition.

A team should ask itself some fundamental questions, such as what is the promise according to our value proposition and what must we deliver to our client relationships? As the team further examines its role, they must also ask, "What is the quality of life that we want our team members to have? Are we providing value to our customers and enhanced service, or are we still doing the things that we've always done? Also, does the team have succession strategies in place? Will the team have sustainability long after the exit or retirement of a senior team member?"

Has the team identified some characteristics that lead to productivity improvement? We'd like to think there is plenty for a team to think about in terms of improving productivity that has been described in previous chapters. Then, of course, there's the client retention and acquisition issue. Are we better prepared to retain our clients now than we have been in the past? There is both a direct and an indirect cost of acquiring a new client relationship in terms of time and resources. Teams must ensure through their service model that clients coming through the front door don't exit out the back door. It's too expensive in terms of acquisition costs and potential revenue loss and the loss of referral opportunities.

One of the most crucial and helpful questions to ask is, "Why are clients better served by having worked with your team?" This gets at the heart of the value that you provide. Is the value you provide understood by your clients? Sometimes to get the answer to that question is to *not* have "groupthink" but to go out and have conversations with your clients and ask them what they perceive to be the value in working with your team. You will ask, "What do you believe our value is? What do you feel are some of the differentiated concepts and ideas that we are providing to you as our client?" At a minimum, ask clients these questions, and that will provide some feedback as to whether your team is effective. Digest this information from your clients and determine if you should stay the course or reevaluate a current course of action.

If you have read all the chapters and everything we have discussed thus far, you will find we've covered the items in this checklist of must-haves for every team:

- Team business plan and strategy document: complete with goals for accomplishment.
- Examination of team leadership styles.
- SWOT analysis: examination of team strengths, weaknesses, opportunities, and threats.
- Team vision statement.
- Mission statement.
- Value proposition.

- 30-second elevator pitch.
- Team communication strategies and effective team meetings.
- Team collaboration and the Force Multiplier Effect.
- Forecasting growth and goal setting.
- Onboarding a new team member.
- Team agreement.

Does the team have a business plan and strategy document in place? Does it include goals for accomplishments? More important than just having the written plan and strategy, does the team have the mechanism in place for the review of this document? The team must examine its leadership styles. Do these styles evolve and change depending on the circumstances that the team might be dealing with?

The team also needs to conduct a thorough SWOT analysis: What are we good at? What's the strength of our team? What are the weaknesses? What are the things that we need to improve on? What are the opportunities that exist in our market that we are not taking advantage of or capitalizing on? And are we looking at things that could potentially disrupt our business? What are the threats that could potentially impact how we interface with our clients? The team should sit down and discuss these issues and, most important, examine the key points in a SWOT analysis. Nothing stays the same; things change, so is the team changing according to these forces of change that impact the team's business in the industry? Let's look at these forces of change.

Michael E. Porter, professor at Harvard Business School, described five competitive forces that impact business strategy. Let's understand these forces in terms of team dynamics.[1]

1. **Competitive rivalry:** Inability to raise prices and intense competition. Because of this, teams must establish differentiation by offering improved value and service to counter the impact of the inability to raise prices.
2. **Bargaining power of product suppliers:** The key issue here is that there is no bargaining power for advisors.

They can be selective in using vendor products and negotiate for value-added capabilities such as training and the sponsorship of client meetings. The power of moving to lower-priced alternatives is in the hands of the clients for the most part. To repeat, bringing collaborative advice and guidance solutions to client problems is a strategy that can differentiate teams! Using technology such as CRM tools to establish connectivity with clients is part of the technology tool box.

3. **Bargaining power of consumers:** Understand that consumer behavior may allow them to "vote with their feet" and leave a team or firm in favor of digital advice channels, which is a competitive threat to the industry. Establishing close relationships that go beyond the sale of products becomes critical to team success. Teams should let solutions to problems drive behavior by delivering advice and guidance through an offering of collaborative capabilities or the Force Multiplier Effect.

4. **Threat of new entrants:** The rise of digital advice channels, connectivity through technology, the expansion of artificial intelligence, and research in behavioral finance will continue to evolve and change the competitive landscape. Teams should embrace technology as a complement to their service model.

5. **Threat of substitute products and services:** The barriers to entry for new products and services are high. However, a new generation of Millennials, 77 million strong, are comfortable with the use of technology and mobile as a means of communication as well as access to applications. Due to an aging advisor population, teams will need to onboard junior team members to exploit this opportunity.

The team's vision statement is basically the team's aspiration. It's aspirational. It's the end game. Where does this team dream they want to be in the next three to five years? The mission statement really is about aligning the team to the factors that they're working toward with the client relationships and the forces of change in the marketplace.

The value proposition is basically the team's promise it is making to clients. It is the level of commitment they're making. Here are the questions you should ask yourself: "Do you have the elevator pitch? Have you rationalized what you really do as a team that adds value to your client relationships? Is this team meeting on a regular basis to communicate real enforced strategies? Talk about what's working well? Talk about what needs to improve? Are you having effective team meetings?" Once team collaboration and the Force Multiplier Effect is in place, you will see the characteristics of a very agile team bringing to bear all the resources and capabilities that it has at its disposal.

Is the team forecasting and looking at metrics, establishing goals and finding ways to meet targets, and holding themselves accountable for performance? Has the team discussed how they will assimilate a new team member or the process for onboarding a new team member so that the team really has the function of everybody being strategically aligned? Does each team member understand the mission and delegation of duties and responsibilities? Then, has the team put in writing the things that they hold sacred, the things that they've agreed to for all the team members?

Review the team's agreement periodically, possibly once a year, to make sure everything that was agreed to is being adhered to and reinforced. As the business evolves, the team may have forgotten some of the commitments they made, so the agreement and the plan and strategy document is a reminder of what the group's consensus was when it was started. It's good to go back and make sure that the team agreement is current. A periodic review of that agreement is very important.

Sometimes going back to the team agreement is a reminder of the difficult conversations that took place for the team to get to that state of being a "live team." It's not necessarily the most comfortable process, because the team had to come to grips with differences of opinion and disagreements to arrive at a consensus that will be helpful to everyone. To go back and take a hard look at it might conjure up these feelings of "oh my, we really went through it." Just look, make sure that everything is still being adhered to, and it could possibly reduce or eliminate conflict in the future.

Key Issues Impacting a Team's Success

We believe successful teams are at the forefront of listening, hearing, and understanding client needs. This enables a team to really understand its offering and how it treats its customers, and continue to get the periodic feedback from clients. A team should relay the feedback to the organizations they work with. It could be some unique examples that might occur in different markets. For example, in Florida there are many retirees. They may want their team to pay attention to some of their retirement needs in a unique manner. In markets where there are more entrepreneurs or small business owners, there may be differences in ways to engage those customers.

We also believe that organizations must seek out opportunities to bring teams together and leverage the team's collective wisdom. Teams in and of themselves can maximize opportunities that sole practitioners are not able to match. When you take the collective wisdom of teams in general, they bring a strength to organizations that can be very significant. The knowledge cross-functional teams can provide leads to prosperous and healthy organizations. Teams are a microcosm of what is great about their organizations, but also what can be dysfunctional.

Teams that are doing very well should be encouraged to help develop better teams. After all, working in a teamwork environment and leveraging the collective wisdom of teams and team members can further help develop other teams within an organization. Organizations have an opportunity to examine and inventory team best practices for future development.

According to Harvard Business School researchers, the average team achieves only 63% of their strategic plans.[2] The key issues impacting their success are how well the team communicates, aligns around top initiatives, trusts one another, creates short- and long-term plans, and holds themselves accountable to deliver the results. If all a team does is go through the process of putting together a great plan and a strategy, and then they tuck it in a drawer to gather dust, they haven't really maximized their real opportunity for improvement.

The same Harvard researchers suggest that most organizations know this and yet lack the know-how or discipline to make sure these issues are addressed each day.[3] Success escapes most organizations because their leaders refer to these skills of communication and trust as the "soft issues" because they don't see how the skills are measurable or quantifiable and, therefore, don't believe they are important to performance as more typical indicators of success. Teams need to monitor actual performance versus planned and forecasted performance. Leaders should coach teams on this process and offer resources to those teams that provide the growth aligned with the overall objectives of the business.

The idea is to have the team develop a work experience to overcome the challenges and optimize success. Again, all team management must start with the right attitude, or the right belief and commitment that they want to get better.

The Message

Even with the complexities, teams really are the way to enhance an organization's success. But the process can be learned; it is a journey. We want to help make the journey "mission possible." The book answers several things: One is that teams have gaps, and we try to help team members identify them and help them overcome the challenges. Also, we always think of disruptions and disruptors as being new and innovative technology. But what we are trying to point out is that teams can be a vital disruptor in and of themselves, because they can bring a very strong human element to client relationships.

The potential and future for advisor teams is bright. If organizations begin to think thoughtfully about onboarding new team members to existing teams as part of success and management strategies, then teams can be self-perpetuating for the organizations they work with.

We want the team leader to reinforce the team's strategies even with their various complexities in terms of collaboration and the force multiplier. Whatever your team's performance is today, it can have productivity improvement gains. Teams are about people. Teams have an opportunity to enhance the client experience. They are just scratching the surface in terms of unleashing the power of collaboration.

If you're thinking about forming a new team, adding a new team member, creating a succession strategy, or looking to grow, or even if your team's performance has flatlined, go back and reexamine some of the key points that were brought out in this book.

Memorable Points

It's important to be personal and show vulnerabilities. Team leaders need to sit down and communicate with team members and hear their insights. Don't be intimidated. And don't feel that you're being too touchy-feely. It's important to be able to explain yourself and how you're feeling and the contributions that you want to make – don't feel that "my contributions aren't going to make any difference and they don't want to hear my contributions." I think that portion of this book really encourages readers to understand that their opinions matter.

If the dialogue is positive, a little contentious discussion is okay if mutual respect is part of the process. If teams thrive, organizations thrive.

Remember, teams are not perfect, and individuals are not perfect. They're human beings – we have flaws. It's important to respect differences. That's another challenge for members of a team because you must have patience with people in general and your members and clients specifically. You just must have patience in life. And there will probably be numerous challenges that teams and members will face. If you're all working toward the same end goal, and you are open and honest with each other, you'll be able to sit down and figure all of this out. And you'll come up with a solution to a challenge, especially if it's a dysfunctional team. Worst case scenario: You'll have to let some people go, or dissolve the team, or who knows what might happen, but that's up to the team to decide. It is our hope that we have given the team some of the tools to deal with potential dysfunction and build a successful team.

Team Challenge

Review all the team challenges and create an action plan for accomplishment.

NOTES

1. https://hbr.org/2008/01/the-five-competitive-forces-that-shape-strategy.
2. https://hbr.org/2005/07/turning-great-strategy-into-great-performance.
3. Ibid.

Index

Page references followed by *f* indicate an illustrated figure or photograph; and page references followed by *t* indicate a table